Shyam Benegal

PHILOSOPHICAL FILMMAKERS

Series editor: Costica Bradatan is a Professor of Humanities at Texas Tech University, USA, and an Honorary Research Professor of Philosophy at the University of Queensland, Australia. He is the author of *Dying for Ideas: The Dangerous Lives of the Philosophers* (Bloomsbury, 2015), among other books.

Films can ask big questions about human existence: what it means to be alive, to be afraid, to be moral, to be loved. The *Philosophical Filmmakers* series examines the work of influential directors, through the writing of thinkers wanting to grapple with the rocky territory where film and philosophy touch borders.

Each book involves a philosopher engaging with an individual filmmaker's work, revealing how it has inspired the author's own philosophical perspectives and how critical engagement with those films can expand our intellectual horizons.

Other titles in the series:

Eric Rohmer, Vittorio Hösle
Werner Herzog, Richard Eldridge
Terrence Malick, Robert Sinnerbrink
Kenneth Lonergan, Todd May

Other titles forthcoming:

Christopher Nolan, Robbie Goh
Leni Riefenstahl, Jakob Lothe

Shyam Benegal

Filmmaker and Philosopher

Samir Chopra

BLOOMSBURY
NEW DELHI • LONDON • OXFORD • NEW YORK • SYDNEY

BLOOMSBURY INDIA
Bloomsbury Publishing India Pvt. Ltd
Second Floor, LSC Building No. 4, DDA Complex, Pocket C–6&7,
Vasant Kunj, New Delhi 110070

BLOOMSBURY, BLOOMSBURY ACADEMIC INDIA and the Diana logo are trademarks of Bloomsbury Publishing Plc

First published in India 2024
First published in Great Britain 2021

A catalogue record for this book is available from the British Library.
A catalog record for this book is available from the Library of Congress.

ISBN: 978-93-61318-39-9

Series: Philosophical Filmmakers

Typeset by Deanta Global Publishing Services, Chennai, India

Printed at Manipal Technologies Limited, Manipal

To find out more about our authors and books visit www.bloomsbury.com and sign up for our newsletters

For Ayana, a woman in the making.

Contents

Acknowledgements

Without whom, not: Costica Bradatan, for inviting me to contribute to this series and for being a thoughtful, supportive and sensitive editor; my brother, Ashutosh Chopra, for procuring copies of the movies I needed to view; Satadru Sen, in memoriam, for providing a much-needed goad for completion; Omar Dahbour, Bradley Armour-Garb and Justin Steinberg, for the kindness of that modern rarity, an engaged conversation about this project; Serene Khader, for conversations on intersectionality and feminism; Dilip Menon, for encouragement during the proposal review process; Sandeep Ahuja, for putting me in touch with Shyam Benegal; David Coady, for his insightful reading of a manuscript draft and for talking to me about the movies all these years; Virginia Held, for introducing me to theoretical feminism; Noor Alam, for being, as always, my favourite reader of drafts and companion in movie-watching.

Introduction

For over forty years now, Shyam Benegal has been making movies informed by a rich political and philosophical sensibility and a visible mastery of the art and craft of filmmaking. Though an autodidactic student of Sergei Eisenstein, Vsevolod Pudovkin and Karel Reisz, Benegal is an unmistakably Indian director, making movies about India and Indians in Indian idioms, striving to realize the universal in the particular through established and innovative cinematic techniques that produce not pedantic forays into a self-indulgent aestheticism but deeply serious moral and political works. Benegal's work acknowledges and displays the eclectic influences of diverse literary, cultural and philosophical traditions spanning magical realism,[1] 'world cinema', Hollywood, modernist experimental novels and the Indian epics the *Ramayana* and the *Mahabharata*, which offer Benegal a set of enduring human archetypes and moral themes woven deep into Indian life. Benegal – the son of an Indian nationalist and who grew up watching movies that dealt with 'social issues' – demonstrates philosophy is autobiography;[2] his acute cinematic vision reveals politics arising from disputes, fractures and contestations, not among abstract political subjects but between highly situated individuals, significantly, often women, located in richly specified, identifiable, social and cultural domains. Benegal is a philosopher and filmmaker; these identities seamlessly fuse in his works. In this book, three portions of his accomplished and extensive oeuvre are examined for their philosophical significance; these readings confirm Benegal as a cinematic philosopher of the first rank.

First, an early set of works – unsurpassed by Benegal himself – the 'uprising trilogy', which depicted the resistance of landless peasants and serfs to a historically entrenched feudal system of landowners, and which signalled to a complacent, self-satisfied and self-righteous newly independent middle-class India that revolt brewed in India's hinterlands. These movies were a galling, chastening reminder that much work remained to be done in the fledgling nation besides formally casting off colonialism and installing a new state in its stead. The 'uprising trilogy' showed older social and cultural pathologies persisted in India's rural precincts, impervious to modernity and 'independence' from colonialism; here, 'subalterns' remained feudal property to be used and abused, their bodies beaten and broken, the fruits of their labours not theirs. But the anger of 'the wretched of the earth' could not be restrained and expressed itself in uprisings of varying passion, organization and effects, each inflected by optimism and pessimism about the possibility of change, each helmed by the subaltern. In *Ankur*, substantive revolt remains incipient as we witness its initial flowering via an unlikely pair of agents of change; in *Nishant*, rebellion is expressed in destructive and inchoate form after a long period of acquiescence and 'forbearance' by the serf; in *Manthan*, it is set in motion by 'outsiders' to be carried on and sustained by 'insiders' who have empowered themselves. These movies provide an examination of the life of the Indian subaltern (very often, a woman), and by allowing us to inhabit his (very often, her) gaze, to catch a glimpse of how rebellion may be occasioned; they offer arguments for the moral permissibility of political violence and present a persuasive indictment of the fused foundations of a hierarchical social order of patriarchy, class and caste.

Second, I turn my attention to a cluster of movies which, continuing a theme vividly present in the 'uprising trilogy', showcases the lives of women implicated in struggles within, and against, the 'cages' created by insidious and oppressive patriarchy. This cluster of movies offers treatments of 'marginalized women' – performing women (*Bhumika*), prostitutes (*Mandi*) and older Muslim women (*Mammo*) – those, who by virtue of their complicated location on Indian social peripheries allow Benegal to bring a 'local', intersectional, feminism to the screen. Here, Benegal's cinematic feminism provides the appropriate analytical and evaluative lenses to track the intersections of the public and the private in the lives of Indian women, and their confrontations with patriarchy and sexism within the Indian modalities of caste, class and gender oppression; I draw on the work of feminist philosophers – from India and elsewhere – to inform the sensitive and empirical social and political philosophy Benegal presents in these works.

Third, I offer a critical and appreciative examination of Benegal's interpretation, 'translation' and reimagining of literary works of diverse provenances and artistic impulses. Benegal's ambition here is as vast as the range and variety of his inspirations: *Junoon* takes on Ruskin Bond's novel *A Flight of Pigeons*, set during the Indian Mutiny of 1857, and explores the private dimensions of a public political conflict memorialized in 'official national history'; *Kalyug* offers a rebooting of the *Mahabharata* to explore the corrosive modern manifestation of its moral and ethical archetypes in a rapidly industrializing India; *Suraj Ka Satvan Ghoda*, a cinematic rendering of a Hindi 'metafiction novel' written by Dharamvir Bharti, offers a 'postmodern' exploration of storytelling, memory, fiction, fictional characters, and cinematic truth and reality – Benegal finds opportunities here for a materialist, Marxist critique of the conventional 'tragic love story'; *Trikaal* explores the interplay between time, memory and spirit in a near-forgotten Indian community and induces a fruitful questioning of conventional distinctions between 'grades of existence'; *Kondura*, based on a novel by the Marathi writer Chintamani T. Khanolkar, indicts a retrograde spirituality and superstition and reactionary social forms while sympathetically raising co-implicated metaphysical, moral and political issues. In these works, Benegal's talents as a cinematic interpreter and storyteller produce movies whose characteristic indulgences – outdoor locales; natural light; region specific rural locations; a cast of 'locals' speaking local dialects; detailed depictions of observances of regional rites, rituals and customs; the artful integration of classical instrumental and vocal music; and components of the grammar of 'mainstream' and 'commercial' cinema – never obscure their humanist and feminist concerns, their essentially moral and occasionally reformist impulses.

As a philosophical filmmaker Benegal animates the existential crisis of the downtrodden Indian, the 'subaltern', the serf, the peasant and the woman, in modern India's continuing political and social becoming. By privileging these gazes, by providing them an articulate voice, by allowing his viewers a measure of participation in their lives, Benegal's movies contribute to a deeper understanding of a highly dynamic polity whose most characteristic feature is continued conflict and contestation across its social hierarchies; his works, which are highly specific to Indian regions in their depiction of local mores, traditions, languages, festivals and rites, do not permit glibness in speaking of Indian culture, which emerges on the screen as a rich and deep body of historical practices, attitudes and moral sensibilities. Benegal thus emerges as a serious philosopher of culture in enabling a critique and appreciation of the 'highest' artistic and cultural expressions of a complex polity like India; most prominently, he allows for an inspection of a 'local politics' that emerges where Indian cultural and social forms – the family, the Indian film industry, classical music and dance, rural social hierarchies – intersect with the balances and variations of power that accompany them. The judgements and analyses that are to be directed at these forms, Benegal suggests, must be cognizant of, and sensitive to, the places and settings his cinema so richly and sympathetically describes and annotates.

Benegal is neither a high-theory filmmaker nor a cinematic pedant, and he does not disdain the popular vernacular of Indian commercial cinema;[3] he is a storyteller, polemicist and entertainer whose movies would be less effective philosophical vehicles in unfamiliar idioms. Pradip Krishen, noting 'the aura of radical chic and glamour' of Benegal's films, describes him as 'the first Parallel Cinemawallah to break through to a popular audience'[4] sparking the observation in response that perhaps 'Benegal's *apparent readiness to compromise* . . . separates his praxis from the more radical aesthetic and political approaches of such committed Marxist filmmakers as Mrinal Sen, Ritwik Ghatak and Mani Kaul'.[5] [emphasis added] This 'failure' to be as 'radical' or 'committed' as these distinguished auteurs of Indian art house and realist cinema does not compromise the moral weight of Benegal's cinema nor does it lessen its political significance. By choosing a 'popular' idiom, by securing commercial success without pandering to the 'lowbrow' demands of the studio marketer, Benegal succeeds in introducing a broad cultural appreciation of, and engagement with, the complex moral and political issues his cinema explores. Moreover, his pre-eminent choice of political subject – Indian women of diverse castes, classes and religions in a fundamentally patriarchal society – is best examined and understood via an existent vernacular in 'mainstream' Indian cinema, the family drama, as opposed to an esoteric and inaccessible idiom, which may obscure Benegal's moral and political claims through avant-garde flourishes and indulgences.

Benegal is not an isolated auteur, bringing forth fully conceived and articulated cinematic works in haughty, self-sufficient, isolation (as might have been said of the late, great, Satyajit Ray). Instead, his works represent deep collaborations between a constellation of diverse literary, musical and theatrical talent, producing a genuinely multifaceted and distinctively Indian production. As such Benegal often calls on extraordinary contemporary Indian artists as co-workers, providing them a distinct venue in which to display their wares in a cinematic context. His screenplays have been written by, among others, some of modern India's most politically sensitive writers Girish Karnad, Vijay Tendulkar, Satyadev Dubey, and Shama Zaidi; his movie's songs' lyrics were often penned by the accomplished Urdu poet Kaifi Azmi; cinematography for his earlier works was performed by Govind Nihalani, an ambitious and creative 'cameraman' who became a master of Indian art house cinema himself, whose *Aakrosh* (1980) is plausibly informed by the 'uprising trilogy' and represents a singular cinematic intervention in the political consciousness informed by it; his movies' music was often composed by Vanraj Bhatia, 'an extraordinary and avant garde film composer . . . able to blend folk music as much as Western and Indian classical music'.[6] Benegal's movies represent the realizations of complex works whose cinematic dimensions are enhanced by the arts brought into dialogue with it; these works thus pay homage, too, to the artistic and intellectual culture that has given birth to them. In so doing, Benegal shows how cinema is more than 'stitched-together' moving images on a screen; it is instead a complex descriptive and prescriptive assemblage of meaning and media, bringing together the written, the spoken, the heard, the felt and the seen. The philosophical claims Benegal articulates on the screen are correspondingly complex, befitting the moral, social and political phenomena that are the subjects of his critical, inquiring and normative gaze.

* * *

Benegal's movies embody philosophy in cinematic form; they are expressions of a moral and political philosophy which chooses cinema as its mode of presentation. Philosophical speculation is not a pleasing side effect, a conceit of a cinematic style in Benegal's work; it is the movie itself, an act of celluloid-based rumination about the drama visible on the screen. Benegal's works demonstrate films can be 'intrinsically' philosophical, and not just illustrators of philosophical claims, as he states and *shows*, through his chosen cinematic technique and style, 'claims' conventional texts cannot.[7] For philosophers do more than just state or refute arguments, their intellectual manoeuvring restricted to the statement of premises and the derivation of conclusions. Instead, they offer acute and poetic paradigm-shifting observations, insights, and perspectives; they show how one thing or state of affairs 'relates' to another in many dimensions more than the empirical; they may analyse 'a state of affairs', not in the destructive, decompositional sense but by showing us what has to come together, and how to make a situation 'hang together'; like Wittgenstein, they may 'point' and 'lay things out for us to see'. In pointing to the world, in directing our attention, in bidding us look within the boundaries of a distinctive moral and political perspective, they may articulate a novel vision of the world which brings hitherto unnoticed political, aesthetic and moral dimensions to light. If thought is to 'lay bare the structure of reality' a movie is a laying bare of 'the heart of the matter' as glimpsed in the director's vision, one informed by a personal intellectual and cultural history, a moral orientation, a political standpoint.

In his autobiography *Confessions of a Philosopher*, Bryan Magee writes of an expanded notion of philosophy that seizes on the 'artistic vision' it enables:[8]

> [T]he most important things great philosophers have to give us are to be got at not by analysing the logic of their arguments or their

> use of concepts but by looking at reality in the light of what it is saying. . . . philosophy is about different ways of looking at things: its purpose is not so much of knowledge as of understanding. An original philosopher is saying to us in effect: 'You will find you will understand things better if you look at them this way.' . . . philosophy can be like art. . . . the result is an enhanced perception and understanding of my own world, my own experience, an enrichment of my vision . . . . What one gets from a philosophy consists largely not of true propositions but, more important than that, ways of looking at things, ways of seeing things.

In similar fashion, Benegal philosophizes through and in his movies because they put, on the screen, 'ways of looking at things, ways of seeing things' that make us view 'reality in light of what [they are] saying' and aid our 'understanding' of the world – by embodying, cinematically, a philosophical thesis. This is not mere illustration; this is the claim itself. Benegal's works thus show how crucial political, moral and aesthetic realities can be understood when looked at 'this way' for we gain from his movies 'an enhanced perception and understanding' and 'an enrichment of [our] vision'. Such works of cinema show us how esoteric philosophical speculation may be sparked by the mundane, how the sacred and the sacral exist alongside the temporal and profane. Benegal's work acquires an added significance and moral weight for he brings to us a world whose contours remain hidden, the world of the Indian subaltern, and a culture, the Indian, which has suffered the indignities of being 'promulgated' and 'interpreted' by colonial and exoticizing sensibilities, shoehorned into ideological historical and intellectual categories that render impossible nuanced and sympathetic judgements of its workings.

As works of political philosophy in particular, Benegal's movies avoid the afflictions of rights-based philosophy where political agents are abstract entities identified by 'bundles of rights'; rather, by examination of concrete political particulars grounded in the specific material and emotional aspects of its agents, they bring a highly situated and realist politics to our attention. The task of political philosophy, as Raymond Geuss argues, is not to 'develop an ideal theory of rights or justice for guiding and judging political actions'. Rather, it is to 'understand why real political actors behave as they actually do'. If 'politics is a skill that allows people to survive and pursue their goals' then to 'understand politics is to understand the powers, motives, and concepts that people have and that shape how they deal with the problems they face in their particular historical situations'.[9] Those 'historical situations' can only be understood with reference to the particular cultures they generate and continue to sustain; Benegal's works act as illuminations of the inner workings of the Indian 'cultures' and 'histories' which give rise to 'Indian politics'. Benegal's works show politics, culture and history are co-implicated and co-informing and as such avoid facile moral and political universes, seeking out, instead, studied ambiguity about the Good, the Bad and the Right in political contexts; they demonstrate that cinema 'serves' philosophy by offering 'philosophy in action'.[10] With his acute attention to the psychological dimensions and cultural constraints of the abstract political and moral subject, Benegal shows himself to be inspired by a philosophical tradition that owes much to, among others, Machiavelli, Spinoza, Hobbes, Nietzsche and, looking further afield, to Shakespeare (as the deployment of the 'Henriad' in a diversity of political theory seminars reminds us every academic year).

Benegal's claims to distinction as a cinematic philosopher rest in his showing that politics and morality are cultural forms, too, arising out of material dispensations in particular times and places to find highly specific expression; in Benegal's cinema, the culture on display is Indian, and the politics and morality we witness on display bears a distinctively Indian flavour. Such an insistence on Benegal's placement and situatedness as an 'Indian' director is necessary both to pay notice to the highly specific politics placed on display, a tribute to his political realism, but also to insulate Benegal from imposed, 'external' stylistic norms about the form and content of his political and moral claims and judgements. Benegal insists, not on a facile relativism but on a realist sensibility that bids us pay attention to the specific identities and particular constraints and capacities of the 'political actors' on display.

Part of the intellectual and artistic burden of the philosopher is the choice of medium or philosophical vehicle for the expression and formulation of philosophical doctrine and claims. A philosopher like Iris Murdoch chooses fiction – for instance, the *Black Prince* articulates the obsessive dimensions of erotic love and its moral implications; Benegal is a philosopher who has chosen film. Such a choice has a distinctive philosophical implication for its reliance on a visual medium whose images enjoy epistemic primacy in cultures produced and inhabited by beings whose overpowering sensory modality is sight, who believe 'seeing is believing'.[11] Within such cultural contexts, on the screen, the non-existent, declared impossible by 'truth' and 'common sense', and 'dominant paradigms', acquires life and language; it speaks and commands; it constructs and modifies material realities; to place spirits, of whatever kind, on the screen is to claim these exist and possess 'a measure of reality'; their vanishing from the screen is their 'passing away'. A movie is a vision of an alternative moral and political ontology, a trip to a possible world with imagined contours realized and made manifest. Philosophers glibly refer to possible worlds and counterparts, depicting alternative realities in which existent facts are manipulated to allow philosophical speculation about unrealized possibilities; the director of movies grants us access to these possible worlds with distinctive style and philosophical import. A film then is a thought experiment, a simulation that explores the plausibility of a philosophical thesis, a philosophical device that points to novel political, ethical and aesthetic complexities. A movie is a distinctive space in which to press theoretical claims; on screen, the material and the spiritual interact to offer us a richer, less 'repressed' reality.

The political import of these considerations for Benegal's cinema is that on the screen, those who otherwise lack voices and agency can 'find' them, spinning out a vision of an alternative world in which radical political possibilities are realized; the viewer is confronted with carefully constructed alternative moral, ethical and political contours for the currently realized world. When a movie's peasant strikes a landlord his cinematic violence points to a possible world in which peasants do rise up and strike their oppressors down; on screen, when a woman 'talks back' to her husband, demands sex from her partner or seeks work outside the walls of the traditional patriarchal home, we see resistance made manifest in a concrete, even if imagined, social domain. To see such acts cinematically realized is to see a path of resistance by such political subjects illuminated, to see at least one argument against the possibility of resistance, its supposed lack of conceivability, eliminated. A movie that depicts political revolt by eternally oppressed subjects offers us a simulation of how the rebellion might be occasioned, how it might proceed, its tactical and strategic orientation, its prospects for success, its political and moral failings. A director – like Shyam Benegal – who populates his movies with women who surprise viewers by doing 'non-feminine things', like expressing unbridled desire for sex or being verbally or physically assertive, makes the feminist point that such behaviour is unexpected because we have been conditioned to believe otherwise by our social arrangements and paradigms. Our unsettling, our induced unease, is the reaction required for this philosophical claim – the possibility of resistance to systemic oppression – to find traction and possible empirical realization.

Benegal has claimed, 'We need to see things not with the filter of what is given but to see things as they are.'[12] To disdain the gaze of 'the filter of what is given' is to refuse to succumb to ideological claims; Benegal claims the filmmaker can 'see through' these to see 'things as they are'. Film is thus granted the revelatory power of laying bare the 'realities' obscured by ideology; the mere 'recording' of events might, without critique, swallow whole the ideological pretensions of entrenched social and political power relations. As Max Horkheimer had noted in writing on crude nineteenth-century positivism, 'faithful observers' tender no critical account of the phenomena – the political prisoner in his cell, for instance – that they observe and record in their notebooks.[13] But the feature movie, with its fictional imagination, its provision of a cinematic perspective on the 'existent', brings hidden political articulations to light through its cinematic devices; it is no mere passive observer but an active, constructive, critical interpreter – thanks to the philosophical vision guiding the directorial lens.

Contemporary philosophy's academic variants are elitist, practised by professional philosophers whose work is discussed by other professional philosophers, in fora like universities and academic journals and monographs. Benegal's work, in contrast, privileges 'a domain of Indian politics in which the principal actors were . . . the subaltern classes'.[14] By letting subalterns – whether a low-caste man, a landless peasant or a Muslim woman – speak unhurriedly, without interruption or censorship, in the midst of their survival, contestation and resistance, Benegal's work emerges as activist cinema. His philosophical style incorporates a polemical modesty, a refusal to speak for his subaltern characters, choosing instead to portray them as complex, conflicted and situated agents, and not mere instantiators of theoretical claims (a criticism that may be levelled, occasionally, at some of the 'more radical' filmmakers Benegal is compared to). Benegal thus lets the viewer 'work through' his cinematic offering rather than stepping into a didactic stance; no woman or peasant polemicizes; there are no monologues that rehash feminist or socialist talking points. We do not attend sermons; we witness lives lived on their own terms, within their own material and emotional constraints. We are not tempted to sermonize either; the rich, intimate description on display bids us instead to pay *attention*, to *notice*, to *listen*.

Critical appreciations of Benegal, paying heed to his location and placement in 'modern' Indian realist cinema, his funding, late in his career, by the National Film Development Corporation, ascribe him a 'state realism'[15] or 'developmental aesthetic'[16] characteristic of the Indian 'new cinema' of the 1970s.[17] In these assessments, Benegal appears a state-funded, largely conventional filmmaker committed – like the Indian Constitution – to 'secular' and 'universal' claims, to making films 'closer to our sense of reality, closer to the Indian experience, closer to the kinds of lives we lead'.[18] But Benegal's truly distinctive positioning within long-established Indian traditions of realist and political cinema – embodied, for instance, in the works of Bimal Roy, Guru Dutt and Satyajit Ray – is that he is a feminist, and an intersectional one to boot. This is not just a matter of his explicit theoretical claims like 'gender equality automatically represents massive social change'.[19] Rather, Benegal consistently offers us a 'woman-centred' cinema that produces powerful personal statements by, and about women, their sexuality and liberation, and their role within Indian society; in Benegal's movies women are 'intelligent, powerful, purposeful, determined, yet humane and compassionate', thus offering a significant feminist claim against the dehumanization of women by patriarchy.[20] There are no insignificant women characters in Benegal's films; even movies without women as central characters feature women who play important roles in their narratives, crises and resolutions; this placement is of significance in making women *visible*. By virtue of this prominent presence of women in his movies, his respect for the particularities of women's differences and their demands for substantive moral and political equality, Benegal commits himself to the strong claim that women are always *present* and must be reckoned with and heard – in both the public and the private; the subaltern who speaks the most, the loudest and the most clearly in Shyam Benegal's movies is the Indian woman.

1

Poet of resistance
The 'uprising trilogy'

Shyam Benegal's moviemaking career began in the 1970s, as India emerged from the shadow of its first prime minister Jawaharlal Nehru's reign, as populist revolts, armed uprisings – often suppressed by military action – and in a spectacular act of political self-mutilation, a government-imposed suspension of fundamental constitutional rights, the so-called Emergency, placed Indian democracy under a spell of existential questioning. The lenses Indian writers, poets, artists and filmmakers turned on India during these years enabled an acute stocktaking and reckoning of its continuing moral and political development. For these introspective efforts often offered an unflattering, searing counterpoint to the nationalist and patriotic self-congratulation that had greeted the first twenty-five years of Indian independence. Now, contrary to its earlier loftier assessments as an instrument of deliverance and harbinger of a new, qualitatively different polity, the Indian Constitution was broadly understood as a failed 'social contract that did not . . . end the prevalent feudal order' whose most pathological manifestations were 'appalling poverty . . . rampant corruption',[1] and intractable conflicts arising out of 'caste, linguistic, and communal hatreds and passions'.[2]

Benegal's 'uprising trilogy' is framed by this post-independence 'national disappointment'; it critiques the failure of the nascent Indian state to deliver on its lofty promises of a secular, classless republic distant from its older pathologies,[3] as Indian classes and social formations, placed in conflict in an emerging and inarticulate political order, struggled to evolve 'new values'.[4] The uprising trilogy's depiction of the painful, transitional development of social, moral and cultural values arising from these contestations placed Indian liberatory politics in concrete contexts, as India became 'independent' in a sense more actualized than having traded a colonial viceroy for another English-speaking, English-educated lawyer as the leader and architect of its emergent polity. India, as a postcolonial nation, acquired definition through such cinema – it became 'visible'; its moral and political challenges were identified as the tasks of future Indian polities slowly hove into view.

By the end of the 1980s, Indian audiences of 'new cinema' had become painfully aware of post-independence peasant and serf struggles against feudalism and its associated social dysfunctions. In particular, nouveau riche urban Indian middle-class viewers most uncomfortably recognized the India portrayed in Benegal's uprising trilogy. Their treatment of their indigent servants and 'domestic help' – those who cleaned their cars, washed their dishes and clothes, mopped their floors, cooked their food, the ones not allowed to eat and drink out of kitchen utensils used by the upper-caste bourgeois family, whose women were leered at, groped and raped by 'the men of the house' – did not differ significantly from how landlords treated their serfs; the feudal realities of the rural India were replicated in its urban, supposedly 'modern' precincts. As such, the rural rebellions depicted in the 'uprising trilogy' were visible warnings that these revolts could occur elsewhere, wherever tyranny, in whatever shape or form, was manifest. (Benegal does not, however, depict industrial actions, strikes or labour unrest in the 'uprising trilogy'.)

By way of historical resonance, these movies invoke the Telangana People's Struggle (1948–51), a defiant grassroots rebellion for autonomy and self-determination which followed on the heels of Indian independence and left its mark on a young, politically impressionable Benegal – and his nation. The Telangana People's Struggle's causes – feudal reform – and methods anticipated the late peasant Naxalite uprisings led by the Communist Party of India (Marxist),[5] which were to become 'famous' or 'notorious' – depending on your political perspective – for their violent methods of resistance, and for the Indian government's brutal, heavy-handed suppression and quelling of their rebellions. Variants of these uprisings continue in Maoist-Naxalite insurgencies in Indian states today; the transformation of Indian electoral politics to incorporate the voting energies of India's 'backward classes' – untouchables, landless peasants, migrant workers – confirms an 'electoral revolt' is underway in contemporary India even as its current hijacking by the forces of reaction – as manifested in the rise to power of the Hindu nationalist Bharatiya Janata Party (BJP) – continues an unsurprising, if dispiriting, world-historical trend.

The 'uprising trilogy' depicts three different kinds of 'uprisings' with varying visions of change articulated within them; in none of them is the state resisted or overthrown. The state and its formal legal apparatus of governance, when not wholly invisible, appear powerless and ineffective, unable or unwilling to intervene in the microinteractions of the landlord and the peasant 'away' in the villages. These movies helped articulate a deep-rooted suspicion of electoral democracy and its associated politics in postcolonial contexts: that postcolonialism meant the nominal identity of the rulers in the metropole would change while the hinterlands, the frontiers, and the countryside would remain ruled by the owners of historically established material hierarchies who, as collaborators with dominant power, would retain their 'offices' by negotiating new terms of control with the new rulers. (Indeed, despite the expenditure of considerable reformist energies, the material power of entrenched landlords and the new industrialists and bourgeois classes was often ascendant in the newly independent India.[6]) The 'subalterns', in this dispensation, gained little to no power, saw no change in their material realities. Such an analysis suggested that the national exultation over relief from colonialism and imperialism needed to be tempered by an examination of the products of the historical intersections of caste, class and gender in the political contexts of the lands now left free to devise their own futures; there were 'two nations' visible now that colonialism had receded from Indian shores and a politics that was only tractable for one was rendered incoherent.

The 'uprising trilogy' suggests, plausibly, that the first assault on the state, postcolonial or otherwise, would begin with 'minor' acts of resistance that would topple established and entrenched local historical centres of power; from there, the questioning of political and social verities could radiate outwards. Benegal's political vision is thus 'restricted' in its scope but is not lacking in clarity or insight. The 'uprising trilogy', too, by bringing women and their hitherto hidden world to light, struck telling blows for a programme of change directed upwards and outwards from the private hearth and home to the patriarchal public polis. If the state is not resisted in these works, it is because it is implicitly claimed such reform of the public is useless and without political and moral valence, without a more fundamental moral reckoning that must take place in the private. That reckoning would be led by those who, like Mack the Turtle, had been placed at the very bottom of the social order – women, the landless, the lowest castes – but whose 'standing up' could upend it all.[7]

Contra Madhav Prasad – who extends little credit to, or imagines little political sophistication on the part of, the many Indian viewers who flocked to the 'uprising trilogy' – their viewer is not a mere voyeur who gains 'access to the fascination and power of spectacle of feudal oppression and rebellion without being reminded of its proximity in date and time'.[8] If anything, Benegal's work reminded the Indian viewer little had changed since the identity of the rulers of New Delhi passed from British to Indian: the 'new India' behaved and functioned a great deal like the 'old India', and those who left the cities to travel to its rural suburbs knew this well. Prasad's critique disdains Benegal's work as not uncompromising enough in its politics; it accuses him of being committed to upholding a naive political sincerity, a state-ideology-inspired national vision at odds with the pathology he depicts. These political critiques supplement an artistic one, noted earlier, which sees Benegal committed to older, 'mainstream' cinematic techniques. In these understandings Benegal is too conventional and safe a filmmaker, too modest and quiescent in his political claims, to be taken seriously as an activist, polemicist or artist. Benegal's movies, in this view, become part of the state's ideological apparatus, committed to propping up a national sincerity about nationalistic claims. They become claims made by the nation about itself but in a manner that distances itself from the pathology it displays, restricting itself to a removed judgement of disavowal.

The misunderstandings of politics and art in these critiques runs deep; they do not reckon with the manner in which the 'uprising trilogy' was received by its audiences, who saw in its movies an acute failure of the national project, one that implicated its viewers – forcing introspective examination about the nature of their nation and their citizenship – as well as those whose lives and acts it brought to the screen. Benegal's political function is wholly misunderstood if he is viewed as a promulgator of a staid, sincere, naive conception of the Indian nation; the placing of the family and the village as a fundamental unit of Indian political life makes his 'private cinema' devastating and corrosive of established public political verities. If the nation is constructed and constituted by the innumerable private realities on display in Benegal's cinema, then to submit a critical description of them is to do no less than to question the nation and its cultures itself.

The 'uprising trilogy' is often referred to as the 'rural trilogy' in extant critical writings on Benegal; the physical and moral geography of 'the Indian village' depicted in them is a far cry from the romanticized and idealized village of mainstream Indian cinema, which depicted idyllic refuges from urban life, or the blank canvases of reformist visions. If the nation of India was understood to be a largely rural one, then this highly particularized cinema of the village was no less than an identification of the 'real India' which was to be the subject of political theorizing and praxis. The true significance of the 'uprising trilogy' is that it was made in a postcolonial context, questioning the national project underway for its failure to be genuinely inclusive in a manner befitting its theoretical and rhetorical pretensions. This failure was most visible when the fundamental unit of Indian life, the rural weekday, received its dues on the screen.

Ankur

Benegal's international award-winning debut *Ankur* (The Seedling, 1974) recounts the rise-and-fall tale of a young landlord Surya, who is forced by his father to move to the village from the city to manage his family's ancestral property. There, on the feudal estate, he finds his own 'heart of darkness' as he alienates his tenant farmers and the local community in manifold fashion and sexually exploits a tenanted Dalit woman Lakshmi after humiliating and punishing her husband, Kishtya, who promptly exiles himself in disgrace. Finally, after callously abandoning a pregnant Lakshmi, as Surya subjects her now-returned husband to a guilt-stricken brutal assault, we see the feudal estate reach its proverbial tipping point and prepare to 'shrug off' the landlord; a 'seedling' of revolt has been planted, there to bring forth the fruit of defiance.

Ankur applied 'psychological realism' to select mainstream Indian film industry conventions,[9] a stylistic marriage of craft and convenience that paid dividends at the Indian box office and introduced Benegal's work and 'message' to a larger audience; it featured, in a stunning debut, Shabana Azmi, who would become one of India's greatest screen performers, and two veterans of Bombay theater, Anant Nag and Sadhu Meher, in its leading roles.[10] *Ankur* borrowed its conceptions of the lecherous, leering, exploitative landlord and the eternally oppressed feudal serf from older Indian realist cinema – especially the work of stalwarts like Bimal Roy – but by situating them in a particularized regional and intersectional aesthetic brought the true social dysfunction and brutality of their unequal relationship to the fore. In its frank exploration of the hitherto invisible and misunderstood sexuality of Indian women, it contributed, too, to a politically and socially significant informing of patriarchal Indian moviegoers. *Ankur* was shot on location, in specific regional settings, and eschewed conventional devices such as song and dance sequences, a distinctive signature of Indian mainstream cinema; its actors speak in Dakhni, a local dialect of Andhra Pradesh, and participate in regionally specific rites, rituals and practices, rendering a visible locution of their location in space and time and instantiating Benegal's claim that 'the more culturally specific you are, the more universal you will be'.[11]

Ankur depicts a bildungsroman of sorts for Surya, a member of an older feudal order, one corrupted by its landed power; ostensibly a secular and egalitarian visitor, an enlightened messenger bearing tidings of reform from the modern city to a backward village, he soon shows himself to be a retrograde reactionary. His father, the archetypal patriarchal landlord, subjugates his idler heir, committing him to manage the precious bounty of his landed properties; Surya, who has resentfully and unwillingly borne the brunt of this paternal power, does not hesitate to impress that power on others, to exercise the 'rights' his father has exercised in the past. Machiavelli would have disapproved of this 'prince' and his crude displays of power, his cruel expressions of a counterproductive and corroded moral and political sensibility, his corrupted *virtu*; they signal a moral and tactical failure to recognize, and empathize with, those who inhabit 'inferior' social orders of caste and class. His arrogance and resentment are 'naturally' and dangerously directed at his father's erstwhile mistress and her son, his half-brother, his lower-caste serfs, the local villagers, and the village policeman. Surya professes not to believe in caste and older social forms for his own convenience – as in accepting a cup of tea brewed by his low-caste female serf – for he is not a reformer. He kicks the local priest's animals off his land, refusing to let them graze as an informal courtesy, and does not let his father's mistress and his half-brother access irrigation water in the neighbouring fields; there is a rhythm of life, an ecology, in the village, and Surya disrupts and destroys it. This disruption is expressed vividly in Surya's attempts – bumbling and awkward, and arrogant, self-entitled and selfish – to sexually exploit Lakshmi and in his cruel, formal and informal, assaults on her deaf-mute alcoholic husband Kishtya. Crucially, Surya is resisted by the woman Lakshmi, whose manifold defiance clears the way for the seedling of revolt to be planted.

For Lakshmi, in cinematic and material terms alike, is the 'real boss'. A diligent serf, Lakshmi is the de facto estate manager as she works on the fields, grinds spices, cleans, cooks and chases stray cattle away. Lakshmi is loyal to, and protective of, Kishtya, her friend and companion; her relationship with Kishtya is not circumscribed by its sexual bonds and has failed to produce a child – an absence that does not diminish their relationship's emotional affects. Lakshmi grants Kishtya a measure of agency by seeking and procuring employment for him, by shielding him from the psychic abuse others would direct at him. Surya, enthralled by Lakshmi's visible sexuality and agency, covets her and seizes an opportunity to publicly humiliate his 'rival', Kishtya, after he is caught stealing toddy liquor from the estate's palm trees. An angry and mortified Kishtya flees the estate, and in his absence, Surya and Lakshmi's relationship is sexually consummated. Lakshmi becomes pregnant; the cowardly, contemptible and callous Surya, worried about his local reputation and paternal wrath, 'asks' Lakshmi to get an abortion. Lakshmi, at her most defiant, rejects his attempts to purchase her silence and acquiescence. The appalled local villagers – as their leering speculations suggest – acknowledge Surya's right to use the bodies of landless women but expect him to maintain a genteel propriety, to pay them a maintenance income and a grant of property like his father did; an older noblesse oblige had kept Surya's father, and significantly, the villagers too, in line. Surya rejects this possibility for redemption within the feudal framework; his corruption by feudal power has induced a moral and strategic blindness. From his vantage position of caste, class and gender, Surya cannot discern the moral failure visible in his exploitation and abandonment of his 'lover'.

These developments set up *Ankur*'s dramatic conclusion, a cluster of climactic scenes of philosophic brilliance: a sober Kishtya returns home and gives Lakshmi his hard-earned money, proud of this visible evidence of his personal, self-directed redemption; he is ecstatic to find she is pregnant, naively imagining her incipient child is the result of their sexual life. Kishtya takes Lakshmi to a temple to give thanks to the local deity, and then crosses the fields, walking quickly towards the landlord's house to ask for work to support his growing family. Kishtya's purposeful walk, stick in hand, is misunderstood by the watching Surya, whose mind, trained by patriarchy and feudalism, interprets Kishtya's actions as those of a rival, now come to assert ownership of a 'property' misused by another; he responds with an act of nervous and fearful violence. Benegal cuts to a shot of milk boiling over as Surya attacks Kishtya and beats him viciously with a knotted whip; his wife Saru, other serfs, the policeman and his half-brother, symbolic of the public and private in the village, are an appalled audience. But Lakshmi, who has come running to Kishtya's aid, intervenes, placing her body between the cowering Kishtya and the raised whip; she curses Surya as she hands out a fierce tongue-lashing, unrestrained by older reticence in the face of feudal power:[12]

> You hit him, you bastard? Why did you hit him? He was only coming to ask you for help! Did you feel guilt in your heart? Were you scared? We are not your purchased slaves! We don't want your work or your money, or anything of yours! You will never be happy with the sighs of the poor on your soul. You beat my man; the Lord will beat you!

Surya is overcome by shame and flees back inside the safety of his home, to tearfully cower behind a closed door – even as Saru, seeing his mortified and terrified expression, realizes what has happened between Lakshmi and him. As the beating halts and as the tongue-lashing continues, we catch a glimpse of a previously unknown, barely articulated world, one in which a child resists the unquestioning internalization, the unblinking acceptance, of feudal power. As Lakshmi and Kishtya leave, limping away to their waiting home, still tenants of their master and lord, a young boy who has been watching

Kishtya's beating and Lakshmi's defence of him throws a stone at the landlord's house, shattering a window: the unjust and cruel beating of Kishtya has introduced a moment of stark clarity for this young political actor. The boy's stone throwing, clear and decisive, shatters the graveyard quiet of the estate; its uneasy peace is disrupted, without compunction, for the landlord who had ruled with such an unrelenting iron hand for so long.

The boy's stone throwing is a scene of cinematic brilliance in its conciseness and expressiveness; a deliberately chosen act of violence breaks through a barrier imagined sacrosanct but which cannot resist the anger of the oppressed; the serfs have entered a previously inaccessible domain of political agency and choice. The dramatic awakening of the previously quiet is Benegal's strongest cinematic move; the stone-throwing boy, visible as a witness in earlier scenes of Surya's behaviour, has given no indication he is susceptible to revolt and rebellion. His awakening has been prompted by continued, and finally, unbearable evidence of the landlord's brutal dominion *and*, crucially, by the fearless resistance of a woman. The boy is 'the seedling of rebellion' against the landlord's power; he is history's witness and actor, making a new India come to being; he is an impressionable child, not an adult who has succumbed to the supremacist ideology of the landlord. The screen turns red – perhaps a flag for a political ideology, perhaps an indicator of the gathering storm – as the closing titles flash up on the screen. The fate of the 'uprising' remains unknown; though Lakshmi and Kishtya return to their hut, an apparent status quo, a fatal rupture has taken place.

Lakshmi's defence of Kishtya is considerably complicated; when Surya had first punished Kishtya, he was an old-fashioned enforcer of an accepted feudal law, his secret lusting for Lakshmi not directly apparent; in his latter incarnation Surya is a malevolent 'sinner' who projects his guilt on to 'her man'. During the earlier punishment,

Lakshmi had not identified with Kishtya; during the later one, she does. When Lakshmi acquiesces to Surya's sexual demands or lets him humiliate her husband for stealing, she is complicit in and accepting of an established power, which has impressed its ideological claims about the sanctity of feudal property and the all-encompassing reach of the feudal lord upon her. The spell of that power is broken, decisively, by its signalling it is not bound by the moral imperatives that animate Lakshmi. Then, Lakshmi knows Kishtya is falsely punished because of her 'infidelity', bringing her to his defence; her actions do not offer systematic, organized resistance to the landlord but rather a spontaneous defiance channels and focuses a dormant anger arising from the preceding humiliations sent her way. For Kishtya's earlier punishment was directed at Lakshmi as well, an unsubtle reminder of her 'bad choice' in marrying an infertile, low-caste drunk – no matter how loyal and affectionate. Importantly, since then, she has received personal confirmation of Surya's moral worthlessness – directed at her most prized personal possession, her unborn child. Now personally affronted, overcome by shame at her 'betrayal' of Kishtya, a shame that co-indicts Surya as her corruptor, by an anger that has identified Surya as a crucial oppressive, destructive force in her life, she strikes out. This is political resistance, but it is not informed by a theoretical manifesto as much as it is by personal affect.

Ankur crucially places the progressive empowerment of Lakshmi in sharp and acute contrast with Surya's corresponding moral decline; the decadent feudal system brings forth the upstart subaltern in the presence of the right kind of oppressive counterpoint. The various displays of Lakshmi's competence and independence in her work on the feudal estate find their counterpart in portents of doom – the local villagers speak of 'a rotting rope' – that suggest the days of the landlord are numbered, that the landlord's power is an archaic, decaying one, soon to be displaced by the visible dynamism of the awakening serf. Lakshmi's gender and outcaste status, her 'twofold subalternity',[13] subject her to intersectional oppression, but Benegal's camera and script persistently privilege her agency, allowing her to raise her voice literally and figuratively in the various vivid depictions of her work, her sexuality and, finally, her uncompromising anger directed at Surya.[14] A subaltern woman thus reclaims power through words and action; by acting, by resisting, she demonstrates 'the subaltern *can* speak'[15] – even if Lakshmi's 'transformation' is local, restricted and unsystematic for she is not the torchbearer of a larger movement against Surya's landlord class. Still, her defiance is public, and on view, a fact of considerable significance in *Ankur*'s conclusion and in gauging the possibilities for further uptake of Lakshmi's anger by the village's residents.

The least empowered woman in *Ankur* is the upper-caste woman, Saru, Surya's wife, who graphically demonstrates the intersectional flavour of Benegal's depiction of the relationship between characters nominally united by gender but separated by caste and class. Saru's 'resistance' to the patriarchy that has married her off to Surya is limited to oppressing a supposed mate in gender solidarity; she freely asserts her upper-caste privileges in establishing her station at the feudal estate. On arrival at her husband's home, Saru's sexual jealousy is immediately provoked on encountering the active, attractive and dynamic Lakshmi; she spends an awkward first night with Surya, the presence of the absent Lakshmi palpable in their marital bed. To assert her higher-caste privilege within the fine-grained taxonomy of the Indian caste system, Saru refuses to accept tea made by Lakshmi, who is of the potter caste. After Lakshmi's morning sickness announces her pregnancy, Saru expels her from their home and kitchen, and glibly but truthfully claims they will find someone else for household work; there is no shortage of serf bodies to press into the service of the landowner. In this callous disposability of the Dalit woman, Saru cannot see Lakshmi as a fellow traveller, someone bound, like her, by patriarchy's strictures; instead, she views her through the lenses of sexual jealousy and caste and class distinction.

Saru and Lakshmi are both 'women', but Benegal asserts here that Saru's gender, though bearing much in common with Lakshmi's, is distinctive: it is that of a higher-caste woman. There are no sisterly, empathetic conversations between Saru and Lakshmi; the interactions between a poor, low-caste woman and a richer, higher-caste woman are thick with mutual distrust and suspicion. When the pregnant, tired and lonely Lakshmi steals food from the estate's kitchen out of desperation, Saru catches her and proceeds to castigate her, 'You steal and that is why you die of hunger!' Her chastisement is the scolding of the self-righteous powerful, who find virtues lacking in the hungry bodies they have oppressed and induced desperation in. Saru does not say, as she well might, 'You are dying of hunger, so you steal.' Saru can direct the hostility of her sexual jealousy through the weapons of caste and class; lacking a comprehension of the material relationships between gender and caste and class oppression, Saru maintains a studied distance from the absence of choices in Lakshmi's life. Saru can only direct her aggression passively; she lacks concrete, material agency in her married life and freely lashes out at Lakshmi in efforts to assert it; but it is Lakshmi's anger, directed at her husband, which causes her to realize that Surya's violent bluster of ownership masks the guilt of the sexual and physical exploitation that has betrayed the vows of her marriage.

Lakshmi's anger is liberatory for a woman who is not a fellow passenger; it will enable Saru to renegotiate the terms of her relationship with Surya. Benegal's subversive point here is that women, who as Simone De Beauvoir had noted, are unlike any other 'ghettoized' class for being isolated in their political silos, unable to form alliances with other women, can find feminist solidarity once they are made witness to the anger and resistance of other women. Such anger reminds them of their own precarious locations within patriarchy; the resistance on display points to the way out.

Two crucial set pieces in *Ankur* lay out Lakshmi and Surya's understanding of their sexual encounters, their framing of their roles within them. In the first, Surya and Lakshmi witness a card game whose denouement replicates that of an infamous sequence in the *Mahabharata* in which the Pandavas' eldest brother, the virtuous truth-teller Yudhishthira, gambled away his wife, Draupadi (whose husbands included the other four Pandava brothers), to his malevolent cousins, the Kauravas, after a series of losing wagers; thus was woman affirmed as patriarchal collective property by the greatest Indian epic of all. In *Ankur*, a drunken villager, having lost all in reckless wagers to his friends, continues to gamble and proceeds to 'lose' his wife to his mates as a demonstration of his 'manhood', manifested in his stubborn refusal to leave the gambling table in response to their taunts. Surya is ironically nonplussed by this behaviour, for his growing attitude towards Lakshmi is that she, too, is property to be used and discarded.

In the second, which indicates Lakshmi's 'priming' for her sexual encounter with Surya, another subaltern woman, Rajamma, asserts desire and agency outside the bonds and constraints of marriage, daring to transgress social boundaries twice over by leaving her husband *and* taking up with a man of a lower caste in a neighbouring village. Rajamma is accused of adultery by her husband, her brother-in-law and father-in-law, and is literally dragged to the village panchayat, there to be denounced and put on trial. At her public hearing, the unrepentant and indeed, brazen Rajamma defends her actions with her provocative statement that her husband is impotent and that she desires a child. When reassured she will be taken care of by her propertied in-laws, Rajamma retorts that her appetite, which is 'not only of the stomach', remains unsatisfied. This assertion of her sexual desire, her not-dormant-sexuality, is crucially unconcerned with the protection of fragile male insecurities and of the preservation of patriarchy's existent social orderings. Her in-laws rightly fear this desire in suggesting she will induce 'doomsday' with her demands;[16] its assertion entails the disruption of that social hierarchy which has allowed them to physically and psychically dominate her. The watching Lakshmi is simultaneously appalled and intrigued by this display of defiance by a woman whose station is not dissimilar to hers. Crucially, she has witnessed male desire placed in counterpoint to the female variant and noticed the latter not back down: womanly desire can speak and assert itself in public spaces – there to be viewed, interpreted and internalized by other women.

Surya remains as unaware of the effect of Rajamma's words on Lakshmi as he does of the conclusion of the card game he had witnessed earlier. For when the reckless gambler's wife finds out about her husband's wager on the morrow as the irascible friend shows up to 'collect', she contemptuously rejects his claims and loudly scolds her husband in a comic scene which depicts her as a house-ruling shrew. Both subalterns' actions in the private sphere thus disrupt an older established narrative of the public; here, private, domestic politics feature different power relations than those of the public; here, small, private resistances counter oppression through the voice and deeds of a supposedly repressed and silent subaltern. In these depictions of a woman's rejection of patriarchal control of her body in a traditional space, Benegal supplies a feminist rejection of totalizing narratives for oppression, making room for the recognition of battles not showcased in traditional accounts of resistance in the public sphere. He suggests, too, that women who offer public displays of resistance empower other women, forming 'shadow' or 'hidden' alliances whose effects may not always be immediately manifest. Such a depiction of the effects of the public resistance of women allows for an understanding of Benegal's movies themselves serving as models of resistance for their women viewers – and as warnings to men that their private fiefdoms play host to not fully acquiescent and potentially rebellious women.

As Needham notes, Benegal's treatment of the sexuality of his women characters in *Ankur* is modernist in its implicit claim that acute social transformations follow when women are liberated from specifications of 'normative and deviant sexualities'.[17] For Benegal's frank depictions of Lakshmi and Rajamma's sexuality counter ideologically inflected claims that such women are 'un-Indian', that female sexuality and resistance is an outlier, an affront to established patriarchal reality and its norms of sexual propriety.[18] Benegal's women character's sexuality counters, too, conventional depictions of Indian women in Indian films where their characters are simultaneously virginal, chaste, sexually innocent, unrelentingly 'faithful', yet charged with hypersexuality in formulaic and risqué musical song and dance routines. The resultant oppressive 'idealization and fetishization',[19] a distinctive feature of Indian patriarchy, 'bind' Indian women, leaving little space for personal agency in sexual choice and expression.

Lakshmi's 'sin', most prominently, is to display sexual agency in her relationship with Surya and her refusal to perform as an erotic oddity for his male gaze. Lakshmi is not concerned to make herself attractive to Surya, to use her sexuality as a weapon; her pride and defiance, ironically, are her sexual allure. When she does succumb to sexual desire, we see little evidence of genuine romantic attraction to Surya; she is instead driven to seek a 'mate' who can give her the child not forthcoming in her relationship with Kishtya. Later, as Lakshmi worries about the social realities that will keep their 'forbidden' relationship illicit and hidden, Surya glibly speaks of defying convention; a sceptical Lakshmi maintains a distance from such fantasies for she knows caste and class separate her from her landlord. Despite her sexual relationship with Surya, Lakshmi remains protective of Kishtya; she defends him against Surya's attempts to demean him as an ignorant deaf mute, and glowers angrily when questioned about his possible infertility as a reason for her childlessness; if Lakshmi is guilty of 'infidelity', then it is a considerably more complicated notion than the notion of an 'unfaithful woman' suggests. We, the audience, do not see Lakshmi as a 'betrayer' of Kishtya: How can this strong, beautiful woman stay faithful to a man who cannot do justice to her sexual desire?

Still, the possibility of 'rape' hangs over this sexual relationship's ambiguous consents: in fundamentally unequal social contexts, 'under conditions of male dominance', rape and intercourse are 'difficult to distinguish'.[20] For a serf like Lakshmi, whose body is owned by feudal power, intercourse and rape may blur; here in feudal society, where sexual exploitation of serf women is 'routinized beyond denial',[21] Lakshmi's acquiescence is plausibly informed by fear of expulsion from the estate, and subsequent impoverishment, were she to refuse Surya's advances. Lakshmi and Surya's 'embrace' finds its balance of power resting on Surya's side, whose reductive gaze directed at Lakshmi fixates on her as an object of sexual desire. But Lakshmi's sexuality complicates the condemnation we direct at Surya, for while Lakshmi seems incapable of sexual consent, we sense a sexual agency that desires personal 'completion' through pregnancy. She has been exploited, but she has, too, exploited the landlord's body, drawing from it the 'sustenance' she needed.

Elsewhere too, Benegal's sympathetic depictions of Lakshmi powerfully question dynamics of power between genders and classes; Lakshmi is always portrayed as an active agent, whether attending to housework, tending the fields, rejecting Surya's evasions and cowardice, and most dramatically, becoming her husband's protector, subjecting Surya to a verbal assault as damaging as a physical one. When a snake appears in the fields, Lakshmi handles it with confidence and aplomb; in sharp contrast Surya appears out of his depth and is content to let her 'take the lead'. Lakshmi does not dance; she does not sing; she is not concerned to 'market' herself as a ware for her feudal lord. And Surya and Lakshmi's sex remains off-screen, as Benegal refuses to provide titillation to the male gaze.[22] Lakshmi's revolt is vividly revealed, too, in her refusal to have an abortion, her resistance to being a 'mere kept woman' to be used and discarded when convenient. As she cuttingly reminds Surya, she does not ask for, and does not expect, his support in any shape or form; when Surya calls out to her as she washes herself at the banks of the river, she spits out the water in her mouth, eloquently.[23] (Benegal emphasizes that Lakshmi's gender is not a handicap in her relationship with her lower-caste husband; within her caste, within the four walls of their hut, she can assert herself, as she must, with exasperation and impatience, when, all too often, the drunken Kishtya straggles home. Out on the feudal estate, she is less able to do so.) Lakshmi's roles – breadwinner, protector of men, her laughing at Surya's clumsiness in his attempts to aid the work of the estate – establish her favourable placement vis-à-vis the supposed locus of power, the male landlord. She is oppressed, but she is not an acquiescent, collaborative slave, and she does not lack a voice, figurative or literal, with which to resist.

As Needham notes, by the placement of his lens, by focusing on Lakshmi's actions and words, Benegal makes the viewer an accomplice in her gaze directed at Surya and her world.[24] By being able to perceive her complex public psychology, we come to understand her inner world too; Benegal thus introduces to us unheard and unseen subjects and their political consciousness.[25] This visibility is of acute moral and political significance; it is, after all, Lakshmi's gaze that makes the cruelty directed at Kishtya visible.[26] What else might we come to notice were the gaze of the subaltern to be privileged? Which new world's contours would become visible?

Patriarchy and feudalism persist because both the oppressed and their allies, men and women across class and caste divides, have 'learned and inhabited various modalities of domination and subordination'. *Ankur* suggests such internalization requires 'sustained long-term effort to unlearn'[27] and offers a clear-eyed vision of how such emancipation might begin, even as its future contours remain to be determined by further uprisings and contestations.

Nishant

Nishant (The End of the Night, 1975), starring Amrish Puri, Naseeruddin Shah, Girish Karnad, Anant Nag, Smita Patil and Shabana Azmi, implicates patriarchy and violence with feudal power in a pessimistic narrative that shows an 'outsider', a school teacher, a supposed educator of untutored minds, introduce a fatal disruption in a zone of feudal domination.[28] Within its confines a brutal landlord and his dissolute younger brothers run their property with an iron hand, dispossessing and oppressing their serfs, freely abducting and raping the local women; their invasive, totalizing control extends to the kidnapping and abduction of the teacher's wife, who is imprisoned and sexually assaulted within the walls of the feudal estate; the teacher, unable to find succour and 'retrieve' his wife through the state's legal avenues of power, instigates and leads a rebellion against the landlords with tragic consequences.

In *Nishant* feudal power is a social and economic arrangement underwritten by established schemes of patriarchy and masculinity, which rely on the subjugation and seizure of male and female bodies as modalities of control in the emasculation and enervation of their landless subjects. When the feudal lords gleefully evict and humiliate a delinquent tenant, forcing him to kneel and grovel while his children watch, we see their brutal exercise of power is as erotic to them as their violent domination of women. Their guiding principle and motto, which runs together sexuality, violence and feudal power, is proudly announced as, 'Land and women must be controlled with force; otherwise they will become someone else's.' These imposed feudal burdens prove to be intolerable and provoke a morally justified act of political violence; even if this retaliatory 'rebellion' does not overthrow a state, it crucially signals a limit to the oppression the subaltern will countenance. And to the extent to which the subaltern's anger will be confined by external normative assessments of the propriety and appropriateness of the form and content of his resistance and rebellion. The subaltern knows, better than anyone else, the true reactionary intention behind the pious calls to channel and direct protest through the 'correct' and 'appropriate' forms of resistance: the preservation of extant forms of power.

The radiating centre of iniquity in *Nishant*, the landlord's household, is populated by four brothers – Anna, Anjaiya, Prasad and Vishwam – who are united by misogyny, by a masculinity founded on the domination of their bonded tenants: male serfs massage and groom their bodies and till the fields while female serfs serve as involuntary sexual providers. The bristling, powerful, eldest brother, Anna, is the brutal, enforcing, face of his feudal power: after he orders a peasant's crops seized, Anna kicks the plaintive mercy-seeker aside; when villagers come asking for release from eviction or the burdens of rent, he summarily dismisses them from his presence; the villagers hold their heads and weep stoically for these states of affairs are familiar to them. Anjaiya and Prasad conduct another reign of terror in the village; for them women are mere objects, their physical attributes the only dimension of interest for them. The village's pathological power relations permit the brothers to command a peasant worker to send his wife to their home to be raped; the wife learns her emasculated husband cannot defend or protect her. When we see the serf woman next, she is putting on her clothes; she has been used, violated and abused by a half-clad, drunken Anna while Anjaiya and Prasad await their turn. For the brothers, women are sexual beasts of burden reduced to their physical particulars; the serf women whom they take turns sexually assaulting are dehumanized objects, recipients of an unending stream of psychic and physical abuse. The younger brothers note that the head of the household, Anna, presumably a role model and aspirational ideal for them, never bothered to 'bring a domestic cow home', preferring 'the milk of the cows of the market'. Such beasts of burden are not worthy of moral attention or sympathy; they are understood to be incapable of speaking up, of self-assertion – a misunderstanding that will be removed by the actions of the subaltern.

Conventional conservative sociological wisdom claims the absence of patriarchs in households contributes to a higher crime rate and a culture of criminality; Benegal shows homes without women who resist patriarchy offer fertile breeding grounds for toxic masculinity. On the feudal estate, there are no women to provide a countervailing moral force to the perdition that rules within its walls: the younger brother Anjaiya's wife ran away; the older brother Prasad's wife committed suicide; we may reasonably conjecture she was abused and driven to death. Vishwam, the youngest, is married to Rukmini, who offers sporadic critical commentary on his dissolution, occasionally acting as a displaced moral conscience; otherwise, she acquiesces to the depredations of the men of her household, desperately and unsuccessfully seeking to normalize the pathology witnessed in her daily life. In this fraught space, a physically and morally weak man like Vishwam, mocked and scorned by his brothers, is able to exert his will on the unwilling, to 'be a man', to take his turn to abuse women; he is made physically sick by the liquor forced on him and morally sick by his acceptance of their ill-begotten gifts.

Nishant functions as a powerful feminist work by documenting misogyny, by showing an indispensable component of male power is the objectification and exploitation of women who find their 'sexual parts or sexual functions ... reduced to the status of mere instruments'.[29] But despite documenting sexual exploitation in *Nishant*, Benegal does not explicitly depict rape, refusing to provide titillation to its viewers; in patriarchal societies cinematic rape is scarcely innocent in functioning as a brutal revisitation of original trauma. Benegal emphasizes instead a woman's 'subjective perception' of the violence of rape;[30] on screen, the rape *Nishant* depicts does not evoke reactions conditioned by patriarchy but empathy with its victim, for we do not see the perpetration of the rape but the response to it by its victim.[31] And indeed, one woman, Rukmini, the daughter-in-law of the feudal household, with little power to change the material realities of her life on the estate and who tacitly accepts the teacher's wife's abduction and confinement, mocks Vishwam by asking whether his masculinity and manhood have been demonstrated by his complicity in sexual assault, and demands to be sent back to her parents' home. She glowers and backs away from a 'defiled' Vishwam, thus reversing the usual schema by which a woman is 'violated' by rape.

In *Nishant*, we witness the world-building, consciousness-sustaining power of feudal ideology and its inhibition of 'normal' human agency. The landlord's power is an ever-present feature of the villagers' lives, for by systematic and sustained application, and not persuasion or formal indoctrination, it has utterly conditioned the villagers' thought, speech and action. Nietzsche had imagined the creation of a sovereign self through repeated punishment of the individual, through searing into its temporally extended memory, a persistent, enduring pain only assuaged by debt repayment.[32] Here, the landlord's power has, through the sustained exertion of cruelty over time, impressed into the villagers a nominal self which unblinkingly obeys the landlord – it knows and remembers its previous punishments and it dare not speak up, for fear of incurring the same agonies that have been visited upon it previously. The obsequious village policeman (the symbol of the power of the state), the meek temple priest (the earthly representative of divine power) and the timid villagers (children of the gods and wards of the state) all collude, in their own fashion, with feudal and patriarchal power. The village policeman's formal legal power is subservient to, and functions as the spear tip of, the landlord's power; law acts here as a compliant, compromised enforcer of reactionary political ideology. In this village, children, in their mimicry of adults in their 'innocent' games, take on roles in which they invest themselves with the oppressive power of the landlord, displaying familiar patterns of behaviour reinforced by observation.

The collusion of the villagers with the landlord follows from their internalization of the ideological structures of feudal power, for the feudal brothers' routinized amoral pathology provokes no condemnation or rebuke from their subjects. As the feudal serf well understands, under oppression, conventional understandings of human motivation, action and responsibility break down; 'normal' agency is replaced by pathological stasis, a failure to resist. The physically and mentally subjugated feudal subjects the landlord's power and reach has produced, the local villagers, are impervious to the moralizing hectoring of the teacher when he demands their help in rescuing his abducted wife; they have shut their ears to their consciences, reduced to the most basic of desires to stay alive; these are agents in only a nominal sense. In this zone of totalizing domination by the landlord we find the transformation of human agents into 'zombies'; for the landlord to be resisted, a new self must be created.

But no programme of systemic change produces such a new self; rather, one man's resentment, fear and shame are channelled into an explosive, all-consuming demonstration of rage that breaks older moulds of acquiescence. *Nishant* is keenly perceptive in showing the true locus of resistance to the landlord lies not in political subjects' response to programmatic political appeals but in lower-level psychologies; the isolation of the villagers from larger political realities ensures their resistance is not provoked by a systematic political platform. Instead, an emotional, and at times, shaming, appeal is made to their sense of rage, humiliation and emasculation, with moral lessons drawn from the transparent moralizing of ancient epics. At *Nishant*'s bloody climax, the procession which brings the soon-to-riot villagers to the landlord's threshold commences from the village temple, home of transcendent, categorical, moral orders, patiently treading a path of justice that finds its violent terminus at the feudal estate's doors.

A set of crucial opening segments establishes the all-pervasive power of the landlord in his 'kingdom': *Nishant* begins with the sounds of prayers in the dark; the land and its peoples are cast in darkness, awaiting the 'end of the night'. A preliminary screen title, placed at the insistence of overly sensitive Indian censors, 'insists' the events to be depicted took place 'in a feudal state during the year 1945' and clumsily attempts to absolve post-independence India of the social pathology we are to witness. This little bit of political prudery only served to remind the Indian viewer of how the interior of India represented a time warp impervious to modernity. A priest walks up the steps of a temple after completing his bathing rituals; as this holiness in human form emerges, accompanied by music that portends doom, he makes the shocking discovery that the temple idol's jewels have been stolen. Many Indian myths and legends feature wrathful divine retribution directed at humans whose actions test the limits of the patience of the gods; *Nishant* begins with such an act of defiance and defilement, moving into the realm of Indian myth and fable as it does so. The priest, hand shaking, finds a familiar locket; we cut to Vishwam waking with a troubled expression; he has lost his locket. The villagers bring news of the robbery to Anna as he receives a massage from a labouring slave. The feudal lord brusquely disclaims responsibility and directs the meek, acquiescent, villagers to the ineffectual and uncaring police. Anna reassures his worried brothers, the temple's robbers, who had sold off the temple's jewels to settle their gambling debt, that he will secure the locket; here is the real seat of power in this land. (A limit to feudal power is found in the moneylender's collection of debts; before this material, financial reality even the landlord must bow.) A scapegoat, a local beggar, is found, duly indicted, and beaten by Anna as the gathered villagers silently watch an ancient scene of punishment and retribution. Anna promises the priest the temple's repairs will be completed by next harvest, as will the procurement of new jewels for the idols, by Anna. The priest hands over Vishwam's locket; he is regulated by a power greater than the one prayed to in the temple; he must acquiesce to, and be complicit in, its crimes. The priest's knowledge the jewels have been stolen by the brothers generates an acute incoherency that action is impossible despite the possession of an ostensibly actionable piece of information. The landlord thus defiles heavenly power to protect his property and morally corrupt family; perdition beckons as ancient spirituality gives way to the amorality of profane power. In *Nishant* all is a foretold disaster once the temple, the abode of the gods, is desecrated. (Later, Rukmini, responding to the abduction and 'imprisonment' of the teacher's wife, Sushila, pleads to Vishwam's conscience, 'She is a child's mother; God will not forgive us.' This invocation of divine wrath in an Indian grammar indicates a crucial moral boundary has been crossed, and heavenly retribution awaits. But Vishwam, intoxicated by the sexual power that flows from feudal, masculine possession, does not heed her warnings.)

The feudal brothers' desecration of the conventionally sacral continues with their abduction of the new schoolteacher's wife, Sushila, soon after the family's arrival in the village. In the abduction's aftermath, when white robed villagers silently emerge from the dark to testify to their helplessness, the teacher is finally made privy to the village's terrible secret, one only dimly visible thus far: the power of the landlord is unquestioned and reaches into private domains without compunction. The teacher's attempts to rescue his wife are futile: he rants heedlessly at the gates of the landlord's residence; the police respond with insouciance and languor; the teacher has no witnesses to back up his claims for no one can be persuaded to speak up. The villagers' eyes have not recorded the sight of his wife's abduction; it is not an act visible to them. Formal law is useless in the face of local power; a lawyer informs the teacher he has 'no legal case', that he should be 'realistic' and not go beyond his station, and indeed, 'get [his] head screwed on right'. The local paper refuses to cover the 'story', fearing a libellous accusation without legal heft; more to the point, it fears retaliation by the landlord. Bewildered and tormented by opaque, irresistible power, the hapless teacher goes to the court, a house of the law, seeking the civil services administrator, who cannot 'do anything' till he returns from a tour of his precincts. The seeds of revolt are present in these demonstrations by the teacher that he will not passively accept his fate; they are present, too, in the state's professed inability to protect its wards, in its confessions of helplessness and incompetence.

Away at the landlord's home, Sushila, a sex slave of Anjaiya and Prasad, is not restrained and bound, for no earthly powers intrude to challenge the authority of those who confine her. Vishwam, after initially declining to join the rape of Sushila, attempts to 'seduce' her with a new saree; her path to this new servitude is to be eased by the same transactional sex she had previously 'enjoyed' with her husband. Sushila accepts Vishwam as her sexual partner, finding an attention and novelty denied her in her older relationship; perhaps Sushila prefers this model of masculinity, finding the power and illicit sexuality of her new residence more salubrious than her 'staid' life with her distant former spouse. Most crucially, her husband would not accept such a 'defiled' and 'used' woman; now 'ruined', there is little to be gained by Sushila's further resistance to sexual exploitation.

Besides legal relief, the teacher has found no spiritual comfort, for when he consults the village priest he is recommended a stoic acceptance of misfortune and the theological and metaphysical comfort of the spiritual afterlife as a distraction from earthly pathology. When the priest tells the teacher to 'go to God' and find peace there in repose and worship, the teacher responds that the deliverance of the next world and the afterlife is a fatal invitation to lassitude and passive acceptance of injustice in this one. The priest is fatalistic, resigned to destiny; the teacher is unwilling to bear injustice passively. These 'conflicting views of tradition and modernity, of resignation and rebellion'[33] will find their dialectical synthesis in violence.

But the villagers will not resist spontaneously; their behaviour remains frozen in older moulds of acceptance and quiescence. The teacher and the priest therefore attempt to mobilize them through 'a politics of shaming', directing accusations of cowardice at the villagers, exhorting them to rise up. Revolutionary solidarity is established in the oldest of Indian ways, as the villagers accept new sources of authority to guide their resistance to the landlord: the priest and the high-caste teacher. The villagers respond and are 'followers' again;

this time they seek deliverance, by their own hands, from an alien power that has ruled them their entire lives.

Nishant's closing sequences signal the growing storm, inexorably moving its characters along to the final, fatal resolution of their lives. A villager stares resentfully at Anjaiya and Prasad as they walk by; the scapegoated beggar returns from jail, unbowed and defiant; he spits at the police. The continued insolence and sullenness of the beggar signals resistance never died down entirely in these precincts; the low-caste beggar, the lowest of the low, represents the furthest reach of the stirrings of rebellion. At the village's buffalo jousting festival, as beasts lock horns and clash, the villagers are enthralled by the spectacle of conflict; within this restive crowd, the village policeman feels threatened while the spectators ignore Anjaiya and Prasad who were not formally invited to the event as was the local custom; earlier, as they drove through their fields, the brothers had noticed their workers were absent.

Back in the village, Anjaiya finds their car's tyres punctured and complains to Anna that they have not been invited to the bullfight. Anna remains oblivious to the incipient crisis, but unease stirs. His servant continues to serve Anna, massaging his legs, his expression indicating a novel sullenness. Away at the once-defiled village temple, the priest conducts a ritual ceremony attended by the teacher and the villagers; Anna prepares to receive the procession that sets off from the temple, to fulfil his social role as benefactor and earthly lord. The brothers wonder why no one has come to work, not even their lowly servant woman, Porchamma; her absence signals the psychic and physical abandonment of the estate is complete. Sushila joins Rukmini in the kitchen; their common servitude exposed now that servants have left, their work reconciles them momentarily. The temple procession consisting of villagers singing and chanting finally arrives at the estate's doors; the feudal family prepares to receive the procession, which has brought statues and idols, divine justice, to their doorsteps.

Nishant's ending is stunning and brutal as the gathering storm breaks. The teacher attacks Anna as the villagers riot; an earlier rape victim and the servant woman, Porchamma, are visible in the raging mob that invades the landlord's home. Anna and his brothers know the end is near; the oppressors' fear is visible as they realize the spell that entranced the village has lost its power. The brothers fire their ineffectual guns at the mob, which chases them into the house and lynches them; Rukmini's watching gaze is vengeful, but she is lynched too. Vishwam drags Sushila away from the home and run; they flee to a distant hillock and sink down exhausted and spent; the teacher follows, desperately hoping to save Sushila from the rampant mob. Sushila comforts Vishwam as she realizes the end is near; we see the pain of a mother realizing she will not see her son again. The last grim lynching, on the top of the hillock, is inevitable. Vishwam and Sushila do not escape; the mob swarms over them as we see the first blows fall; there is no mercy, no setting apart 'victims' or 'collaborators' from 'oppressors'; God will sort them out once they are dead. Back at the landlord's haveli, now a charnel house, an innocent observer of the carnage, a young boy, is left looking at the corpses of its former inhabitants. The boy runs away; the priest covers Rukmini's body with a cloth covered with inscriptions bearing the legend, *Ram Ram*. We see children in a room at a temple; they have been watching a play.

In *Nishant*, Benegal's ironic and subversive readings of Indian epics like the *Ramayana* pay homage to their interpretive richness and complexity and demonstrate their affordance of multiple interpretations, their philosophical fertility. Here, Sita (Sushila) abandons her consort Ram (the teacher), choosing captivity with the demon king Ravana (Vishwam), forswearing the captivity of one kind of domestic life for another that liberates her sexuality.[34]

As in the *Ramayana*, the sexual purity of the abducted woman is a crucial plot device; in the *Ramayana*, Ram demands of Sita that she prove her sexual purity and chastity after her extended captivity, a patriarchal challenge to her fidelity and integrity that she defiantly responds to by leaping into a fire – the divine witness, a symbol of cosmic purity in Indian mythology – from which she emerges unscathed; in *Nishant*, Sushila's 'defilement' means she cannot return to her older home even were she to be 'rescued'. As generations of Indian feminists have pointed out, Ram's challenge to Sita is an assertion of male privilege in asking a woman to 'prove' herself as 'worthy' despite having suffered grievous injury herself; Ram's 'rescue' of Sita is not so much as an act of aid or succour, as it is a conditional reclamation of property seized by a male 'rival'. The Sita of *Nishant*, Sushila, is assertive; she complains about the move to the village – analogous to Ram and Sita's exile to the forest – rather than uncomplainingly and passively following her husband as in the original legend. She is desirous of material goods, and amenable to sex under the 'right conditions'; when her husband snuggles up with her in their marital bed, rather than meekly granting him his sexual 'dues', she resists and only succumbs when he accedes to her 'requests' for a mirror and a saree.[35] Benegal invokes, too, the *Mahabharata*'s Pandavas, the five husbands of Draupadi, in Sushila's relationship with her two 'husbands': Vishwam and the teacher. But here, Sushila's rape by three other men complicates our understanding of Draupadi's role and capacities, by suggesting she was 'used' by multiple men, her five husbands. The legendary sage Valmiki's 'hegemonic Ramayana narrative'[36] glorified the rectitude and moral order of the kingly, warrior caste and offered stereotyping images of women as ever-faithful, obedient and sexually pure; in sharp contrast, the warriors here are imperfect realizations of the associated caste ideal, and the women are not chaste, virtuous or ever-obedient. And unlike the *Ramayana*, Sita does not survive her 'rescue'; here, she, too, is punished, for patriarchy's 'protection' of her is identical to her abuse by it.

Violence is central to *Nishant*, the most violent of Benegal's movies, featuring the violence directed at peasants by the landowner, the seizure of the woman's body for kidnapping and rape, the violence perpetrated on her relationship with her husband, and finally, the murderous lynchings perpetrated by the villagers. The retaliatory violence in *Nishant* invokes the militant anti-landlord peasant struggles in Telangana and the brutal violence of the Naxalite uprisings, which included armed battles with police and the beheadings of landlords. But we feel little pity for the brothers; their humanity long lost, they have passed beyond the realm of sympathy. By denying us this affect, Benegal claims the violent lynchings in *Nishant* are morally comprehensible in being motivated by a desire for retribution and 'making whole'. *Nishant*'s associated claim, if the testimony of this indifferent cinematic gaze is any indication, is that when violence comes for feudal power, when the serfs rise to shake off its burdens in as brutal a gesture of rejection, it will not be disapproved of by history. The argument for political violence here is an inevitability claim: there is a limit to human patience with oppression; there will be a time when this patience will run out and violence will be unavoidable, and not subject to our condemnation. There is too in *Nishant*, a carefully described downward arc of violence, not a spontaneous irruption. With formal legal and state power physically and psychically complicit with feudal power, the subaltern subject is left with no recourse: violence awaits.

Nishant does not rely on the trope of a sudden, mysterious awakening as a prompt for the violence it depicts; rather, sacred, unrealized power (the priest) awaits secular power, which must suffer personal injury before being provoked into action; it is the spark required to set the tinder ablaze. The teacher is finally provoked into violence by the shaming of his masculinity, a claim established by Benegal in a sequence that shows the teacher meet his wife – set 'free' as a concession by Vishwam – at the local temple. There, Sushila and her husband do not try to run away; there is no escape. Both display an acquiescence and internalization of the power that oppresses them. The teacher does not embrace Sushila; this is not social propriety but a question of whether someone else's 'property' can be touched; she is no longer his. Sushila accuses her husband of indifference, passivity and cowardice, of failing to act precipitously to rescue her: indeed, she demonstrates she has so internalized the structures of patriarchy that she demands her husband exercise violence to assert his masculinity and 'rescue' her.[37] This, the shaming of the teacher's masculinity by a woman, is the proverbial final straw. The teacher is launched on his path: the rape and abduction of Sushila is a personal affront and his 'resistance' transforms from the need to 'recover his wife' to leading an uprising that ostensibly seeks collective justice against accumulated wrongs. This 'programme' of action is still, crucially, a largely personal one.

The insults tendered to the previously dormant secular and sacral power of the priest and the teacher, the secular and the spiritual educator, are thus established as the preconditions for revolt. *Nishant* devotes considerable time to showing the teacher and the priest provoking insurrection at strategically selected social gatherings of the masses; there, the priest and teacher converse and rabble rouse with the villagers, the beginning of a 'grassroots organizing' of resistance. The political promise of religion is put on display; the priest has long been acquiescent in earthly power, propping up earthly regimes of despotism, passively accepting injustice if obeisance was paid, in the right fashion, in the right time, by humans to a distant god. Now, the tremendous, hitherto unrealized, power of the priest's spiritual, political and cultural capital is directed towards earthly liberation. The promise of liberation theology – that the models by which the gods lived translated into social and political ideals realizable in the world of the here and now – is thereby realized. The villagers listen as priest says that tolerating injustice will not get rid of it for 'Even to eat we have to raise our hands'. As the villagers gather to watch a ballet performance of the *Ramayana*, celebrating the victory of good over evil, the priest confronts the villagers, accusing them of being content to be spectators of battles for justice fought by distant gods – while injustice lives on in their lives; in other gatherings, the teacher invokes the religious epics and their tales of struggles against mythical monsters. We wonder, of course, what, precisely, were the teacher and priest asking the villagers to do? What was their vision of political action? We never hear prescriptions besides 'rise up!' How, in what shape and form? Against whom in particular?

In *Nishant*, at 'the end of the night', the awakening's effects are unpredictable and catastrophic. An empire appears to have been vanquished and swept away, but we wonder about the uprising's resilience. What will happen when the state, which formally and informally supports feudal power, enforces local justice? The logical conclusion to *Nishant*'s uprising is a brutal reprisal from the state and its functionaries, its police and its legal systems, who cannot bear to see extant centres of power – its agents in the hinterland – toppled. *Nishant* and *Ankur* thus both maintain a studied ambiguity about the possibility of social change. In *Ankur*, we glimpse the stirrings, the first flowerings of revolt; in *Nishant*, the rebellion that 'flowers' remains a blunt weapon as it takes on the characteristics of the power it seeks to displace.

For the revolt against violent male supremacist power also wreaks violence on women: neither Rukmini nor Sushila, the women who have borne the brunt of patriarchy's abuses, survive the lynchings; masculine anger is still directed at them for having 'collaborated' with male feudal power. Such a taint on the rebellion we have witnessed marks it as having only made partial progress from the pathology it aims to excise. Benegal's considered judgement on violence as a political tool then is that violence is all-consuming and coarse; it kills Sushila and Rukmini, women who were unwilling collaborators with 'their men', the ones who oppressed the village; moreover, those who previously collaborated joined in the violence, their pasts forgiven now they have 'turned'.

Philosophies of political violence justify and ground it in 'instrumental, necessary, virtuous, tragic or sublime'[38] opposition to the violence of the oppressor, which is found manifested in sexual exploitation, the economic violence of immiseration by the bonded labour of feudalism or the systematic economic exploitation of colonialism. Formal 'wide'[39] and 'expansive'[40] definitions of political violence, which accommodate the violence on display in *Nishant*, suggest that political violence in its feudal contexts is a form of self-defence: violence in defence against violence or in protection of those being assaulted is self-defence against imminent and realized threat. A peasant rebellion and resistance can be a form of virtuous political violence in restoring a 'moral balance' of sorts. The violence in *Nishant* is therefore more than resistance against 'institutional or quiet violence';[41] it is a form of self-defence against the direct and structural violence of the landlord, an understanding that does not merely grant it moral sanction, but also possibly a legal one.

Seeking a psychological foundation for *Nishant*'s rebellion, we find that a defence of political violence like Franz Fanon's, which is redolent with medical terms, may be applied to the feudal context just as it was to the colonial one by Fanon: feudalism carries out 'systemic negation' of the landless peasant and breeds a 'mental disorder' induced by persistent exposure to the 'infection' of feudal rule and ideology; psychiatric illnesses are created for the feudal subject who suffers in body and mind in losing agency; but through violence, the peasant resists desublimation, repression and destructive neurosis. Revolutionary violence is thus therapeutic, for the serfs are 'cured' of their psychiatric symptoms by the 'cleansing force' of revolutionary violence.[42] Violence acts on the self-hatred and impotence of the feudal subject whose fear and resentment of the landlord's oppression have been turned against himself by the repeated brutalization by the landlord; the 'neurotic' self that results can only be replaced by a new one by an act of catastrophic violence. The revolution on display in *Nishant* then reconstructs the old, traumatized self by facilitating physical, mental and metaphysical freedom;[43] the subaltern regains ownership of political affairs as the self damaged by feudalism is restored by violence. So revolutionary violence is destructive in one dimension and constructive in another, for it permits a reclamation of the subaltern's humanity.[44]

The revolutionary violence of *Nishant* is especially cathartic because it is, crucially, action: it delivers the peasant from stasis, and galvanizes him by offering a counterpoint to the endless violence perpetrated by the landlord. In the violence of the formerly oppressed the serf works through self-hatred; in striking back, the serf punishes his oppressor for having dared to subjugate him. The serf thus achieves catharsis through revolt, seduced by the attractions of violence and the pleasures of righteous anger.[45] There is relief for the viewer of *Nishant* too; the resistance of the peasant provides succour to our rage even as we are alarmed by the pleasures of violence. While violence is denied as a political tool by the moralizing powerful to retain its exclusive use for themselves, Benegal shows the subaltern may draw on violence too; the parallelisms between colonizer and colonized, and zamindar and serf, suggest strategies that produced liberation from colonial power, including those of directed, unforgiving violence, will find application in feudal contexts.

Historically, revolutionary violence's constant companion is excess; it releases 'the furies'. *Nishant* is no exception; we are left unsure of what will survive the violence of 'the end of the night'. Following the violence, we do not see villagers setting up a new village council, liberating the serf's debts, parcelling out the landlord's estates to its tenants and evolving new methods of self-rule. What then, will the 'new day' bring? Have the villagers 'learned to resist' so that new feudal power cannot be ensconced? In making violence and resistance serve as a climax to *Ankur* and *Nishant*, Benegal introduces an open-ended texture to their narratives; we are left to imagine what will happen in the aftermaths of the awakenings we witness. Such a directorial choice is deliberate: *Ankur* could have placed its stone-throwing mid-plot to show the gradual decline of the landlord's authority, the pregnant Lakshmi's bearing of her child as a visible and prominent act of defiance; *Nishant*'s violence could have been followed by an extended sequence showing the teacher leaving the village after helping set up local, self-empowered rule. Benegal's ambiguous and ambivalent conclusions challenge our political prejudices instead: Does our political imagination have space for the peasants in *Ankur* and *Nishant* to continue their empowerment? Do we imagine a restoration of the status quo, the law asserting the state's protection of those who own land, the landlord remaining settled in power? Dare we imagine a new world and its contours? This provocation of the imagination by political action, by violence, is Benegal's singular move in *Nishant*. It remains a grim document of rebellion because the revolution it depicts, showing traces of misdirection and bluntness, is not in the right form, and might yet be crushed.

There is no 'systematic' political philosophy expressed in *Ankur* or *Nishant*; their violence is a surface phenomenon, heralding an approaching storm whose dimensions are only gauged when it is too late for the complicit. Benegal thus induces uneasiness in the complacent middle class: look away from the 'evidence' at your own risk; as you verbally and physically chastise the gardener, the driver, the cook, the peon, do not look away from those hungry eyes which conceal a desperate anger, one not to be restrained forever; one day the serfs will break into your house and cut your throat while you sleep. *Nishant* is a pessimistic document of rebellion; but its warnings are clear and unmistakable. Those who ignore them do so at their own peril.

Manthan

Manthan (The Churning, 1976), starring the emerging ensemble of 'Benegal actors' like Amrish Puri, Anant Nag, Naseeruddin Shah, Girish Karnad and Smita Patil, is grounded in the dramatic and still-evolving story of producer-owned milk cooperative societies in India. These originated in the village of Anand, in the Indian state of Gujarat, as a local strategy of empowerment for a historically disenfranchised social group, the landless peasant, often of a 'low' or 'untouchable' caste with nominal 'capital' of livestock, who was economically dependent for sales and distribution on the local landlord – a political economy that worked for those who could leverage local hierarchies of power. These cooperative societies were among the many grassroots-level changes in the Indian polity following independence, including the formal abolition of bonded serf labour and the special rent-seeking privileges of princely states, which were aided and abetted by idealist bureaucrats striving to reform the rural hinterlands of their many pathologies. As a visible demonstration of the power of such grassroots efforts, *Manthan* – whose story is the product of a collaboration between Benegal and Verghese Kurien, architect of India's extensive system of farmer cooperatives – was India's first crowd-funded film, its microfinancing obtained from half a million milk farmers who donated two rupees each to the movie's production budget.[46]

Manthan depicts the intractable politics of reform as external 'reformers' seeking to set up a cooperative milk production society in a remote village encounter its static political reality of entrenched power relations of caste and class. Resistance is engendered as the ostensible reformer realizes he has much to learn himself from those he has come to 'rescue' and as activism flowers organically from local political agents, who empower themselves independently of an 'outsider' whose tenure was destined to be temporary, and whose political and tactical nous is always in question.

Manthan in Indian mythology refers to the tale of the churning of the Ocean of Milk by the demons and the gods to produce the famed nectar of immortality; the demons held the head of a giant serpent while the gods held its tail, pulling back and forth on its body, which was wrapped around a giant mountain, and causing it to rotate. The resultant churning dredges up a lethal poison from the depths of the Ocean of Milk, which could destroy all of creation and must first be consumed by Lord Shiva before the nectar of immortality can be accessed by the gods. In *Manthan* too, the 'churning', the restlessness, the rising, of the dispossessed is not a benign stirring of quiescent, placid depths; it may produce lethal objects with deadly effects. The churning produces the insolent spirit of insurrection but also reactionary violence; the upstart peasant's stirrings provoke the landlord's deadly, retaliatory anger. The resultant fear underwrites the tension and dread persistently visible in *Manthan* as we see subalterns resist a force which has never hesitated to enforce its stations, its hold on power, with unforgiving ruthlessness.

Manthan's opening shots quickly establish the dysfunctionality of the hinterlands. After a train arrives at a rural station carrying a 'reformer', a veterinary doctor Manohar Rao, a delayed receiving party asks for forgiveness, for, surprisingly enough, 'the train has come on time'; dysfunctionality is the norm in these precincts. The horse-driven cart which transports the collected party to the village is loaded excessively; here, casual cruelty may be directed at both man and beast. The doctor declines the ride on the overloaded cart and in sharp contrast to his privileged, indolent, companion bureaucrat, walks to the village. Rao has come to establish a cooperative society for milk farmers, an announcement which provokes laughter from the local officials who, even as they agree 'the nation needs principled people', assure Rao that 'things are done differently around here'. This hilarity at the principled naivety of the outsider suggests disillusionment lies ahead. Here, in a fledgling nation, cynicism is rife; its daily discourse reeks of contempt for the principles the nascent republic claims to espouse. Benegal thus emphasizes, critically, the gap between the promise of abstract 'national ideals' and their empirical realization in the form of situated human agents caught up in their psychological and material compulsions.

Soon Rao meets the local landlord Mishra, who mockingly calls him 'a man of principles', describes the villagers as 'children' and makes note of his intimate knowledge of their lives, acquired painstakingly over thirty years. He suggests Rao will leave – like all outsiders do – that his intended cooperative society will fail, ruining Mishra's business and his 'relationships' with the villagers. Mishra reminds Rao that 'You can make things worse. Change does not always bring progress' and offers him a thinly disguised warning to concentrate on 'health and family planning and welfare work'. Mishra's exaggerated rural accent and mannerisms provide a comic touch to this interaction, but his character is acutely menacing; it is with relief we watch this tense, combative yet nominally polite, scene end. But not before it has vividly articulated the contours of the conflict – between familiar, entrenched power and external, upstart power – that lies ahead. Mishra's lines delineate a clear conservative world view: the 'local' arrangements of the village work for those favourably placed in its hierarchies, and they will not take challenges to their power kindly.

The politics in *Manthan* is small scale, the power dynamics local and intersectional, driven by class, caste and gender conflicts. The brash reformers of Rao's team are urban and scientific, uneasily ensconced in the village; the villagers are reluctant agents of social and political change. When Rao's co-workers arrive at the village, honking their vehicle's horns, driving at breakneck pace through rural roads, we sense discordance, a pessimistic note about the prospects of reform; can political change come in such frivolous, ill-fitting form? Rao and his team of 'reformers' face the onerous task of selling the new cooperative society to the villagers, of explaining to them the astonishing fact that the *sisoty* is literally theirs. The co-op's entry requirements are egalitarian; social class is to be checked at the door and property ownership is not required; the lowest of the low, the untouchables, the Harijans, men and women alike, will be accepted as members with voting rights; the leadership of the society will be decided by a members' election, so the nominal head of the village, the high-caste sarpanch of fifteen years, who owns twenty-five buffaloes, cannot automatically lead. The sarpanch joins, offering platitudes about the virtues of collective work, but protesting the presence of the Harijans; he enforces separate lines for Harijans at the society's office, perpetuating the village's caste-based dysfunction; the sarpanch professes the principle that 'everyone should know their place to improve things for everyone'.

This political crisis of the struggle between the entrenched power of the landlord, Mishra, and his agent, the sarpanch, and the lower castes – *Manthan*'s central preoccupations throughout its narrative – is dramatically emphasized by an extended sequence depicting the cooperative's election of a leader. In preparation, a cowherd, Bhola, formerly stubbornly and angrily resistant to the idea of the society, but now a new convert to its principles, delivers a stirring polemic to his fellow Harijans, urging them to seek power through a new political process:[47]

> Enough is enough. We cannot go beyond our station, but I will fight. You can cower like your ancestors if you want. No benefit will accrue to us if the sarpanch comes to power; we poor people must band together and make our own society; we must have our own representative who will think of us.

At the election a historically entrenched centre of power topples, as the Harijan candidate is elected; the Harijans celebrate while the sarpanch, crestfallen, humiliated and disbelieving, rages against the accursed ephemeral and insubstantial society, which threatens his tangible material power. The sarpanch's tearful resentment powerfully captures the dangerous humiliation and shame at the loss of power that infuses reactionary politics; the society has succeeded in empowering Harijans, but it has tendered a fatal provocation to feudal power.

The revolutionary election result moves *Manthan* to its climax for it provokes immediate blowback in the form of violence – the setting alight of their thatched huts – directed at the village's Harijans. This reminder of the landlord's power – a depressingly familiar scene from Indian political life – brings the Harijans literally and figuratively to their knees. To add insult to injury, the police cracks down on the Harijans as instigators of arson; Rao speaks up for them with verbal advocacy, but crucially, it is Mishra who 'delivers' material comfort for he pays the Harijans' bail to purchase their allegiance. Bhola angrily rejects Mishra's entreaties, as the Harijans are paternally addressed like supplicants receiving alms,[48]

> Our old relationships have been forgotten but I have not forgotten them. Only those are ours who help us in times of trouble. I feel sad for your pain. I have a right to share it; come and tell me your names, those whose houses have burned, and I will help you. Children will make mistakes and the elders must keep that in mind. Now you know milk from water. Anger is not good for you. We have had years of brotherhood, what has the society done for you?

In response, Bhola explodes, hectoring his fellow cowherds,

> We have not come to listen this nonsense. This society is ours, ours! We made it. Only the outsiders have left. Our society, made up of us, remains. We will make it run, all together! We made mistakes, but we have a chance to make something new!

This said, he strides off; a small boy and a woman follow. Mishra describes Bhola as having 'lost his mind', his reason destroyed, and indeed, in this extraordinary and powerful scene, we witness a subaltern losing his older mind. By placing two stirring polemics in the form of Bhola, Benegal emphasizes that while reform has been 'introduced' by Rao's team, it has only taken root when nourished by the words and actions of those who have empowered themselves.

Though Rao and his team must leave the village after receiving new orders, the 'churning' has stirred up resistance: the society's offices are open, and milk is still being collected for sale and distribution; the sarpanch sees a procession of villagers headed for the society's collection centre. Change is afoot, literally, and the older power knows it. The 'churning' has produced new forces and agents of change, of unknown capacities and powers; we may choose to invest ourselves with hope. There is no happy ending delivered by external agents of social change; change comes through the 'stirring' and 'churning' of the local subaltern, with political agency invested in the lowest of the low.

In *Manthan* there is no radical reform effort directed at the state (here understood to be the source of benevolent, benign 'upliftment' programmes). The state is invisible, replaced by the landlord, the high-caste sarpanch, the husband, the representatives of feudal power, caste power and patriarchy; the hinterland is a singularity, a zone of lawlessness, where the state and its laws do not intrude to disturb these historically established centres of power. Change, even if limited and local, will come first through local agents who understand the workings of local power, and who have been most impressed by it. But not instantly, or easily: the villagers are used to conventional foci of state power and imagine the cooperative's founders to be politicians asking for their vote in exchange for promised benefits. The villagers scornfully note that they do not need empowerment but material assistance, for they rely on Mishra for milk sales *and* loans – at usurious rates of interest, naturally. In a commodified society, politics, the sustenance of community, the provision of mutual aid and the desire for empowerment are luxuries for subjects reduced to the fundamentals of existence; their political alliance will go to that formation which promises them material deliverance. The villagers speak the language of an older politics of patronage and paternalism; the reformers seek to inculcate a measure of self-reliance and, consequently, material political empowerment. But such deliverance is not easily 'accepted'; it must be 'owned' first. The reformers struggle to combat the paternal residue of an electoral democracy, which suggests citizens hand over political agency to their 'elected representative'; the society's reformers' idealistic and self-professed aim is to empower the villagers through a combination of mutual aid and collectivity.

It is not political argument, persuasion and organizing that win over the villagers but something else altogether: the doctor's team gains the village's trust in the most old-fashioned ways, by providing much-needed help as distraught parents seek medical treatment for a sick child. Despite the vet's protestations he is not a medical doctor, they insist on his providing treatment. Slipping into the role of an official healer over the ethical concerns of his co-workers, Rao administers an injection and writes a prescription slip; a new relationship with the villagers begins as the child survives.[49] News spreads of the 'doctor' and his powers; now, villagers come to be admitted to the co-op. Change begins in response to an act of healing; this creation of trust opens the door to a sympathetic response to the politics of reform and collective action. Pure ratiocination and the systematic presentation of political arguments would have been ineffective tools to practice politics in this domain. Benegal's inclusion of this scene is deeply significant in reiterating his realist political principles: the levers of political power are worked by a 'local solution', by actors best placed to exercise them.

In *Manthan* the outsider sows the seed of reform even as he fails in his own attempts to induce dramatic change, fatally handicapped by his own otherness, his distance from the lives of those whom he would help. *Manthan* vividly depicts an intractable clash between 'political pragmatism' and 'political idealism', between their normative claims for the pace, form and content of reform. By focusing on the profound inner complications of a political movement striving to change an established polity, Benegal is able to demonstrate theoretical political philosophy must cut its teeth on empirical reality; *Manthan* shows how severely impoverished theoretical descriptions of this space for political change would be that eschewed intersectionality, especially when the 'targets' for reform – the local villagers – are riven by internal divisions of caste. (There are no less than five castes in the village.)

Change in the village's political realities means a displacement of material power and its associated social orderings, but any putative empowerment is limited by archaic relations of feudal dependence and caste and patriarchy.

Political activism is thus stymied by older political formations; it is not enough, or even possible, to set up a cooperative society without fighting feudalism, caste and patriarchy – concretely manifested in Mishra the landlord, the sarpanch and the husband of Bindu, a feisty Harijan cowherd woman. (Like Bhola, Bindu is a reluctant convert to the society.) Mishra is angered by the formation of the cooperative society and seeks to show the cowherds they have not lost their old resource; their rejection of Mishra's new solicitations is emboldened by the presence of their new ally, the doctor. Rao's reformers anticipate Mishra's opposition but not his tactics and are frequently outmanoeuvred by him as he disrupts their work through repeated interventions. The high-caste sarpanch seeks to assert an old hierarchy in his continuing brusque and rude behaviour towards the Harijans; he is the visible, official enforcer of the landlord's rule, one whose power is created and sustained by the landlord's foundations, and who will not hesitate to preserve it.

Patriarchy too resists, for Bindu is prevented from forming alliances with Rao by her jealous husband who seeks to protect his 'property', to circumscribe her behaviour and her social interactions. Bindu though, is not acquiescent, and fights back: when her husband seeks to assert his conjugal rights in bed at night, she fiercely resists him. As he accuses her of adulterous relations with Rao, she spits at him in disgust. Her husband is emasculated by the power of the landlord; humiliated by his wife's visible interest in the visiting doctor, he retaliates, poisoning Bindu's buffalo, killing her livestock, impoverishing her and, later, preventing her from speaking to Rao. Bindu's husband imagines his sexual rejection is caused by Rao, and he is correct, for Rao embodies an alternative, quieter, less demonstrative, less authoritarian model of masculinity, one found attractive by Bindu. Rao and Bindu's interactions are animated by a frank sexual charge, but Bindu's curiosity about his personal life and Rao's clumsy attempts to avoid her questions provoke her hostility. Rao's response is to withdraw wholly from contact with Bindu; fatally, for his political activism, by ignoring a potential ally, he communicates his inability to aid her, to transcend the established modes of behaviour in the village, which are subservient to established centres of power. A potential political alliance thus founders on the treacherous shoals of sexuality and Rao's confused understandings of his political and personal 'responsibilities'.

The villagers and the reformers' mutual misunderstanding is most visible in the 'failed romances' between Rao and Bindu, and between one of his team members and a local village girl. The local girl is seduced by one of Rao's co-workers, and becomes the source of 'disgrace' for her family, a familiar tale for the village, for Bhola is the offspring of such an affair: his mother was sexually exploited by a construction contractor who took a servant woman as his due. (Benegal's invocations here of the sexual exploitation of women in 'service' roles continue the concerns visible in *Ankur* and *Nishant* and continued in *Kondura* and *Trikaal*.)

Bhola and Bindu, representatives of the village's Harijans, are oppressed then by the troika of patriarchy, feudalism and caste relations; little social change is possible in the village if their political dynamism is caged; their resultant distrust of, and hostility to, 'outsiders' articulate a fraught dimension of the reformers' work. Bhola – who angrily resists the reformers' solicitations, claiming the society is 'for the big people who hold us in contempt and treat us like dirt' – and Rao's uncomfortable relationship is symbolized vividly in Bhola's refusal to help Rao push his jeep out of a pothole, sullenly unwilling to be an ally on this collective project. As he insists on seeking Bhola's participation in the cooperative enterprise – Rao notes that without Harijans there is no meaningful conception of 'a co-operative society of milk producers' – Rao is accused by his team of compromising the society's establishment. His co-workers caution him against offending the village's caste sensibilities, personalized in the sarpanch's reactionary attitudes; the local conflict between high-caste villagers and Harijans is a concern not aligned with the co-op's ostensible 'mission'. But it is never clear to Rao (or *Manthan*'s viewers) whether his team's objective is the nominal formation and establishment of a cooperative society or a reform of caste, class and gender pathology. This awkward question may be asked of any 'partial' political reform which avoids 'radical', foundational critique; Rao is well aware he could return to his headquarters having announced the 'successful' formation of a rural co-operative society, one still dominated by the older power of the landlord and his unofficial agent, the sarpanch; such a society would have done little to address the inequalities it sought to reform.

Benegal's critical lens never wavers in its focus on the complications present in the character of the supposed reformer, Rao, whose character offers adequate testimony to the difficulty of finding fully realized political archetypes. Rao is pushed and pulled by competing political interests and personal motivations: Mishra wants him removed as a rival for power; the sarpanch seeks nominal, meaningless change that will preserve his place in the local pecking order; the Harijans are understandably suspicious and unconvinced, disillusioned by the false promises of electoral democracy; his own idealism compels him to seek out bold political alliances; the caution of his group bids him seek pragmatic compromises for fear of worsening village caste disputes; his wife, with her own well-established caste prejudices, disdains the Harijans Rao seeks to empower. (Rao's wife is not content to stay in this remote village in a small house, complains he is too attached to work and suggests Rao empathizes with the villagers because they consider him 'a big man'. This cutting remark insightfully suggests a petty politics motivated by personal aggrandizement; the village may merely be a staging ground for Rao's political 'heroics'.)

Rao's ambivalent dealings with Bindu symbolize his relationship with the village; he is not part of it but keen to draw closer. But if he does, his political mission is destroyed. In his dealings with Bhola too, Rao lapses into uncaring and impersonal responses, too caught up in society formalities to bring a personal touch to his politics. When Rao, after urging Bhola and the Harijans to show political courage and seek election to the sarpanch's post, seeks a nominally attractive political purity by saying he must, and should, remain neutral in the election, Bhola indicts his political agnosticism by noting it supports money and land, real material power, in this conflict. The sarpanch, after all, will retaliate if he loses the election, and Bhola and the Harijans rightfully fear they will not be assisted by the outsider who will eventually, and predictably, leave for 'greener pastures' elsewhere. Ironically, Rao 'surrenders' just as a local centre of power, the new Harijan head of the cooperative society, is elected; Rao, an imperfect reformer, thus abandons the village as its conflicts grow deeper and acquire a critical dynamism, unwilling to account for, and acknowledge, its resident political forces and counter currents in his theory of activism. *Manthan*'s political realism is most visible in this attention it pays to the complex effects of micro psychologies on macro-political realities, in its commitment to the personalities and personal idiosyncrasies of those caught up in 'doing politics'.

Benegal's 'uprising trilogy' finds the 'sweet spot' between a hopeless pessimism – in the Indian context, it might be to plead that caste and rural dysfunction and superstition are such powerful immanent forces they cannot be combated – and a facile optimism. The political awakenings we witness in it are driven by subalterns: a peasant woman, a schoolteacher, low-caste cowherds. The trilogy points out that power is distributed across many loci in a polity and requires local resistance deploying local tactics and techniques. As a work of political philosophy, the trilogy offers testaments to political realism: it inquires deeply into the material and psychological location and identity of political actors and is acutely sensitive to the fine-grained distributions of power that are negotiated by political actors in complex intersectional domains – in the Indian context, this means sensitivity to the dynamics of religion, caste, class and gender. The 'uprising trilogy' recognizes that sexual politics is an inseparable component of all liberatory discourse; political reformation and rebellion of any kind is incomplete without addressing patriarchal power. It remains the high point of Benegal's oeuvre, a remarkable set of cinematic philosophical documents, which nearly five decades on, still offer acute, clear-eyed visions of political liberation.

2

Making women visible
An Indian feminist

Shyam Benegal is a feminist director because his movies represent a sustained cinematic attempt 'to make intellectual sense of [and] critique the subordination of women to men', to reveal its 'moral and political implications', to offer 'visions of liberation' enacted by women.[1] Cinematic feminism is not confined by theory, and lets women's lives 'do the talking'; a feminist movie articulates its theoretical principles by narrative form, by pointing to the states of affairs feminism resists; such a directorial imperative privileges a woman's gaze over conventional mediated-by-patriarchy gazes. In these important senses, Benegal's work is resolutely feminist; his movies about women and their lives reflect a 'predilection' compelled by an 'awareness of woman's centrality to life and society'.[2] Benegal's work constructs the foundations of a cinematic and philosophical anthropology and sociology of Indian women, permitting a sensitive, appreciative and yet critical glimpse of the moral and political heart of the cultural practices his movies bring to life; these feminist documents make 'women a focus of inquiry, a subject of the story, an agent of the narrative'.[3] Benegal's movies embody, too, a central feminist attention to how women resolve the quotidian challenges of patriarchy with distinctive acts of resistance; in so doing, in indicting structural, domestic patriarchy, he exposes the fatally compromised foundations of the weekday, the 'normal', the 'established', the 'commonsensical'. Criticisms that Benegal shows women as 'victims' – a critique he rejects[4] – are misdirected; feminism itself might well be subjected to the same critique for exposing the systematic social subordination of women.

First-wave feminists concentrated on formal, procedural, political and legal equality, 'procured' from the state by conventional means of legislative and street activism; second-wave feminists argued women's inequality is constructed by the promulgation and maintenance of 'unquestioned norms, habits, everyday interactions, and personal relationships'[5] and demanded more exacting scrutiny of the weekday; third-wave feminism indicted these earlier 'waves' on grounds of incomplete representation and insisted feminism in the 'West' be informed by the feminism of the 'rest'. Benegal's second- and third-wave feminist cinema shows feminism has 'local flavours', which struggle against home-grown, oppressive, structural and institutional forces. Benegal's focus on private, intimate patriarchy in complex *Indian* contexts – characterized by interactions between long-established caste, class and gender hierarchies – makes him an *intersectional* third-wave feminist, committed to maintaining 'feminine difference' across global placement while 'demanding' substantive political and social equality for women.

For Benegal's movies are not 'simple' feminist texts, they show that woman 'is not born, but rather becomes a woman' with a twist: the woman is Indian, 'produced' by Indian civilization and culture. The Indian feminism she invokes and responds to is singular, because the Indian oppression of women and the resistance of Indian women is. Indian women are oppressed by caste, gender and class, by the feudal and patriarchal, by the accumulated historical weight of social practices written into, and sanctified by, long-established forms of Indian cultural expressions; the actions of Indian women resist, in an Indian idiom, these modalities of Indian oppression.[6] In illustrating these particularized forms of resistance, Benegal's movies show the identity of 'woman' is an intersectional entity with complex implications in 'family, class, religion and other forms of collectivity'.[7] The 'marginalized' women Benegal chooses to depict and make the subject of his cinema – the rural Harijan woman (the potter, the cowherd), the performing woman (Hindu or Muslim, actress or singer), the prostitute – allow for a particularly sympathetic investigation of how class, caste and religion alter the trajectories of Indian women's lives.[8] Western feminism might depict such 'distant' women as frozen in poses of supplication, awaiting deliverance in theoretical and material terms by white saviours, but the women in Benegal's movies are the agents of their own salvation. They are valorized, placed at the centre of a self-professed 'agenda', 'to show that people can empower themselves'.[9] Benegal though, does not depict feminist activism directed at public causes; his women characters profess no programme of 'systematic' social change; they seek 'local' objectives instead. Their reform is directed at concrete, immediate particulars of their lived lives, at a proximal personal relationship or, in a more existential dimension, their own selves, and not larger abstractions like 'the secular liberal state'.

By privileging Indian women's gazes, by revealing elided social realities and histories, Benegal's movies reveal a culture of the secluded and occluded, and by precluding their reductive and simplistic description and evaluation, they significantly complicate our understanding of 'Indian values'. In producing these often-critical notes on Indian culture's placement of women, Benegal is not an outlier; rather he continues an existent tradition in Indian cinema. The marginalized position of married women and their institutional oppression within Indian marriages are, due to Indian cinematic 'family dramas', 'openly acknowledged elements of popular cultural awareness'.[10] The long-suffering daughter-in-law and wife is an archetypal oppressed woman in Indian cinema; often, the agents of her oppression are, besides the patriarchal expectations of her husband and her disposability by her father, other women, most prominently, her mother-in-law and sister-in-law. Benegal's work thus does not sentimentalize or romanticize the Indian family or marriage, a supposedly sacrosanct Indian institution, and the Indian woman's traditional roles of the 'good' mother, wife and sister within it; instead, Benegal's work indicts this corrosive 'glorification', its denudation of the selfhood women may aspire to. Because of the rich, visual, descriptive sociology his feminist cinema offers, Benegal is able to mount a more fundamental critique of the Indian polity and its private precincts than some supposedly 'radical' theoretical formulation may offer, one divorced from the emotional and affective realities of the situations it aims to deconstruct.

Most prominently, Benegal shows 'women's problems' – oppressive genderization, reduced professional and personal choices, repressed sexuality – arise within particular 'material and social conditions [and] particular practices and institutional arrangements'.[11] For instance, in *Ankur*, Benegal's depiction of Lakshmi highlights the 'material' and 'structural bases' of her oppression; Lakshmi was married to Kishtya because her family, consisting of a single mother, could not afford a dowry for a 'better match'; her poverty is a direct consequence of pernicious 'mechanization' which has destroyed the markets and appreciation for Kishtya's handmade pottery.[12] In *Manthan*, Bindu is forced to abandon her potentially liberatory alliance with Rao because her husband kills her livestock, materially impoverishing her, and driving her into the arms of the landlord, Mishra; in *Nishant*, the serf women who are the subject of sexual assault by the landlords must submit on pain of expulsion from the estate and subsequent impoverishment. Moreover, in his depictions of the traditional Indian family, Benegal shows that unpaid women sustain important and valuable labour markets in the private realm of the home. Benegal thus offers a materialist feminist cinema that indicts patriarchy on grounds more comprehensive than misogyny: women are forced into social cages maintained and structured by their material environment; patriarchy acts as a co-constructor and policer of such spaces.

The 'uprising trilogy' indicted caste and feudalism in the private world of the serf woman; Benegal's movies on women placed in the public's margins, those who act, offer paid sex, or sing and dance, indict the pernicious influence of the patriarchal private on the public in showing how its power relations are reflected in the sharply attenuated choices available to those women who dare step out to seek 'a room for themselves'; it shows, too, how the burden of maintaining desirable and valuable cultural forms is borne by those who are not recompensed in material or political terms. In doing so, Benegal is able to offer a foundational critique of cultures founded on and sustained by the systematic subjugation of entire social classes.

Within such cultural critiques, Benegal shows how women are involved in the practice and sustenance of 'national traditions' and how patriarchal agendas are sustained by these 'traditions' functioning as oppressive forces. The conventional, constructed history of Indian traditions produces the reactionary insistence – often woven into supposedly liberatory anti-colonial discourse – that Indian culture could only be preserved, its lost glories restored, if women abided by their historically and culturally defined 'roles' of faithful, devoted, unquestioning, sexually pure mother, wife and sister. This historical demand produces cultural images and understandings of Indian women that 'become both a shackle and a rhetorical device that . . . functions as a historical truth'.[13] This burden is dramatically visible in a movie reckoned as Benegal's most ambitious and finest feminist work.

Bhumika

Bhumika (The Role, 1977), the first Benegal movie to be made from a literary source, renders an explicit feminist statement in privileging a woman's voice, her gaze, twice over, in telling the story of a woman told by a woman. *Bhumika* is inspired by the Marathi-language memoirs *Sangtye Aika* (*You Ask, I Tell*, 1971) of the stage and screen actress Hansa Wadkar, who led a flamboyant and unconventional life in the Indian film industry of the 1940s and 1950s, and whose frank, outspoken autobiography did justice to her colourful life's painful and challenging contours. A 'rebellious individual, a brave woman', indeed, a woman imbued with a proto-feminist sensibility in her critical understanding of her own life, Wadkar acted in over thirty films and died bereft, an alcoholic, at the age of fifty.[14] Wadkar's position was anomalous; a woman who was a 'commodity . . . but also a mythological temptress figure' who used, and was used by, others.[15] Wadkar slept with her older 'mentor', Jagannath Bandarkar, at the age of fourteen; she was tired of being compelled to act by her family and wanted, more than anything else, a domestic life, a servitude that promised her a greater, if ironic, freedom. Flattered by Bandarkar's 'grown-up' attention, Wadkar sought in this ostensible 'sexual liberation' a rebellion against personal and economic exploitation by her mother, herself compelled by dint of economic circumstance to regard her female child merely as a breadwinner. But Bandarkar, a malevolent Svengali and Henry Higgins rolled into one, controlled Wadkar's mind, body and, most significantly, her purse and wallet: he did not allow Wadkar to get or stay pregnant; he started a film production company to control her finances, sold off her bangles and jewellery, and imposed a veritable curfew on her work hours. As Wadkar caustically noted of her abusive relationship with Bandarkar, 'I was treated as if I were a newly wedded bride. That is, I had to wake up early in the morning, sweep, sprinkle cow dung in the courtyard, wash a huge heap of utensils, and cook.'[16] Seeking escape from a 'rebound' relationship, she was beaten by her husband and raped by a magistrate who was to help her escape; she found, like too many women in similar positions, that she was trapped, her life 'a cage within a cage', bound and oppressed by invisible and visible social, legal and cultural barriers.

Wadkar's life, in its central incoherence, captured an essential tension between the public and private, a central feminist concern that haunts classical liberal political theory and its emancipatory pretensions: What is the nature of the political subject on which liberal democracies are founded, of the private on which the public of the modern liberal state is constructed? Is the liberal public, the esteemed polis that makes citizens and humans of us, to be built on the foundations of a repressive private, where away from the 'prying eyes of the state', men may oppress women and their children freely? Feminism insists the fruits of public modernity can only be ours if the private is modern too; the coexistence of the archaic private with the modern public ensures those oppressed by the private remain an underclass which renders hollow the promises of the modern democracy. The liberal order is thus shown to be incoherent with its insistence on the absence of a normative communal order in the private, which, uninformed by the political, moral and legal constraints of the liberal public, grows ever more hostile and inhospitable to women.

Bhumika's title makes metaphorical note of 'the public and private worlds' of Usha, a singing and dancing actress in the

Indian film industry, who plays sharply contrasting roles in these sundered spheres.[17] In her private life, away from the public, she desires traditional roles but also transgresses their conventional understandings and expectations; in her public life on the screen, she plays, and thus perpetuates, problematic cultural understandings of traditional roles of women, the very ones denied her at home.[18] In one scene the transition between the cinematic depiction of a colourful costumed dance number and the empirical reality of a grim, loveless, exploitative marriage establishes this crucial difference – as does, dramatically, Usha's changing into a different saree on arriving home from work.[19] As Usha changes in front of the mirror in her bedroom, we track her transformation from an empowered, sexually charged performing woman at work to a disempowered victim of a money-grubbing man at home. The acute contrast between the glamorous public and the sordid private is reflected in *Bhumika*'s opening sequence as Usha performs a costumed dance sequence at a film studio, enacting a colourful fantasy of romance and flirtation; later, Usha, now changed into unglamorous street clothes, impatiently waits with a smouldering expression outside the sets, her expectations betrayed by an 'unfaithful love' of a different varietal. That carefully constructed fantasy dispelled, she must now deal with the sordid facts of her actual existence where supposed lovers, rather than cavorting around sound stages and proclaiming romance, are content to betray even the most trivial items of faith reposed in them.

The most appalling contrasts between the public and the private are found in the domestic life Usha finds with her on-again, off-again husband, Keshav Dalvi, a pathological dialectic visible in an early segment when her co-star and platonic friend Rajan drives her home from work. There Dalvi, an insecure man racked by jealousy and envy, waits for her, scrutinizing her every move from a lofty balcony. He glowers at her as she enters, asking, 'Why have you come late? Who dropped you off? I brought you home but won't do it again and again.' Usha is defiant, 'You helped me because you wanted my earnings!' Dalvi scornfully replies, 'You think those earnings are yours? I helped you and your family; I made your career. I gave you food when you would have died of starvation after your parents died.' Her angry voice dripping with contempt, Usha retorts, 'Really, are you feeding us too now?' As an infuriated Usha packs her bags and prepares to leave, Dalvi mocks her, 'You'll come back on your knees again. Take your daughter with you; she'll spend her entire life in strangers' homes.' This searing scene masterfully recapitulates Dalvi and Usha's long-standing personal and professional dynamic, and the acute contrast between Usha's ostensibly glamorous life as a screen personality and this sordid domestic haggle over the particulars of their finances and their parenting.

The largest contrast Usha's life represents is between the public life of a newly independent nation, striving to find a new, postcolonial identity, and the private life of its citizens who continue to be oppressed and subjugated by archaic social forms in their domestic affairs. As Usha's life unfolds on the screen, we hear radio news bulletins, announcing the postcolonial India's commitments to secularism and large social welfare projects; but as the new nation changes, Usha's private life remains in stasis, untouched by the dynamic polity 'outside'. What then are we to make of the triumphant proclamations of the 'deliverance and liberation of entire peoples' by anti-colonial revolutionary movements? Who was liberated, and how?

Usha's public life is a story of material and professional success, her private one a series of personal and emotional failures. Benegal's unflinching look at this world reveals the pathologies of domestic violence, forced abortions and failed, unsatisfying relationships – all contrasted with economic empowerment and fame in the world of the film industry and its movies, which by virtue of their marginalized cultural placement fail to bring social 'deliverance' of another kind to Usha. Through her personal and professional life, Usha moves from man to man, unable to control her destiny because of larger material and cultural forces constraining her, a single mother with no economic prospects besides the singing and acting work she has been doing since she was a child. Usha imagines happiness will be found in domesticity, in the company of 'the right man'; her life's harshest lesson is the 'traditional' Indian home will never be hers, that she must make a life for herself on her own. Patriarchy allows her a sexual freedom that works for the men in her life; it does not allow her to transcend her life's emotional constraints. Usha is free to seek out multiple relationships, but she is not free to find happiness within them – like Anna Karenina, she is free to choose her partners but not to be happy. *Bhumika* thus illustrates, painfully, that women are 'psychologically oppressed' when they have 'harsh dominion exercised over [their] self-esteem'.[20] This dominion is one constructed by the Indian family, by Indian society's understanding of the role of 'performing women' and by male understandings of women's roles, capacities and entitlements within patriarchal systems.

Bhumika is, too, an ironic homage to Indian movies and the dynamic Indian film industry, to the changing roles women played in the film industry of the 1930s, 1940s and 1950s, from early mythologicals featuring queens, goddesses and iconic entities like Savitri, a mythical cultural 'role model' and 'icon' famed for her impassioned attempts to rescue her husband from his preordained date of reckoning with the God of Death, and Nadia, 'the stunt queen', a woman superhero who preceded Wonder Woman and Batgirl by decades, rode horses and fought with swords with masked horsemen. In this cinematic homage, which utilizes four distinct stocks of film to indicate the changing eras of Indian cinema *and* Usha's life,[21] Indian women play adventurous roles that mock their tame domestic reality or enshrine cultural ideals whose social manifestations and understandings oppress them in the public and private sphere; they thus actively construct their own disempowerment in these domains. In her screen life, Usha sings love songs of undying passion to faithful lovers, but there is no such grand romance, no 'knight in shining armour', in her domestic life; her characters might fight masked villains with swords on screen, but at home, Usha must sheath the sword of resistance. On screen, she can declaim soliloquies of passion and poetry; in her personal life, her lovers offer lines dripping with insincerity, narcissism and selfishness. Usha's 'domestic' screen roles are stereotypes of the self-sacrificing Indian woman, the archetypes that animate patriarchal understandings of the Indian woman. One movie poster titled *My Child* shows a mother holding her infant, ready to sacrifice herself for its sake; at home, she has little time to spend with her daughter and is forced to abort her second pregnancy. On screen, Usha is a married woman proudly oblivious to the temptations of illicit sexuality; there, she is a faithful and virtuous wife, the archetypal all-enduring, all-sacrificing mother; in real life, she desires the roles of loving mother and beloved consort but finds herself cast as a kept woman or unserious playmate instead. On screen, Usha enacts the legend of Savitri, pleading for her husband's life, unwilling to lose her 'sacred right' to self-immolate as a Sati, unwilling to be 'alone and dishonoured' were her dead husband to be taken away from her; in her domestic life, Usha would not mourn excessively were her abusive husband to pass away.

The cultural legend of Savitri embodies the feminine archetypes that dominate Usha's life; her failure to be an obedient and unquestioning Savitri in real life is her undoing in the private. Fundamentalist religious-political movements portray such 'practices and traditions as "timeless" elements of "National Culture"';[22] Usha's failure to measure up the archetypes established by such mythologies and pathologies is an oppressive burden; the life that results pays witness to a series of attempts to seek shelter and relief from it.

Benegal's non-linear narration in *Bhumika* relies on a succession of flashbacks – each of which visit a stage of Usha's life and return to a spartan hotel room where she has settled herself after leaving her home. (A familiar ritual for her, for 'home' is not where Usha finds comfort.) This narrative style ensures we grieve each instance of Usha's 'lost innocence', experiencing the melancholia of a life not redeemed; with quiet cuts, Benegal captures the tragic arc of life, the melancholic knowledge that at each stage ahead lie Great Troubles. The first flashback, in black and white, transports us into the presence of a young and spirited Usha and her indigent family. Usha's grandmother was an exponent of classical vocal music, in whose arts she provides lessons for Usha; Usha's mother, a former singer, wants to keep Usha from indulgence and professional work in the performing arts, afraid of the resulting social scorn. A palpably older Keshav Dalvi, a neighbourhood friend whose relationships with Usha and her mother feature unwelcome, too familiar 'touching' and remain ambiguous, is present at these lessons. As Dalvi plays with Usha, he 'cajoles' her into making a childish promise to marry him, a chilling foreshadowing of her eventual fate; Usha is used to being coerced, to learning her power over men is limited to seduction. Dalvi steps into a paternal role, taking the precocious Usha to film studios to keep the family financially solvent; a fortuitous break secures her first role. Usha's conflicts with her mother drive her further into Dalvi's arms, into marriage with, and pregnancy by, him. Dalvi leads Usha to believe domesticity, a conventional life with children and a comfortable household, will soon be hers. Usha imagines 'home' to be a refuge; she will find storms rage here too.

For Dalvi, the archetypal abuser, only cares for Usha's earnings and to exploit her young body and talents; he cuts her off from the various relationships, personal or familial, that offer her psychic relief from his many insecurities. Dalvi controls Usha wholly, coercing her to work, denying her meaningful professional and personal agency, speaking on her behalf, accepting invitations for public relations appearances. Usha has the worst of both worlds: she cannot give up acting, she cannot act with the man she was comfortable with, Rajan; she cannot find domesticated happiness at home. She is an exploited slave, working to sustain others by maintaining the fiction, on screen, of freedom and artistic expression.

In one of her forays 'away' from Dalvi, Usha develops a romantic relationship with a narcissistic, nihilistic director, Sunil, who speaks volubly and loudly of his supposed disillusionment by conventional notions of the good life, and offers an absurdist existentialist vision which rejects religious consolation and speaks of 'committing suicide at the right time'. Usha and Sunil plan a dramatic paired suicide – a rejection of the artificiality of the world around them – but despite lofty rhetoric and much posturing about the nobility of freely choosing to end one's life, they do not go through with their plans. Tempted by the unconventional, Usha takes up the life of a mistress with the stern Vinayak Kale, a feudal landlord whose initial rude interactions with her remind her she is unprotected against the diminished social standing of actresses. Kale installs Usha at his landed estate's household along with his unfazed mother, bedridden wife and young son. Ostensibly granted the control of a household, Usha finds it a prison. The untenable illusion of Usha's 'residence' at Kale's home is dispelled when she seeks the use of the family car to but is told it cannot be used without the master's 'permission'. Kale lectures her on how to preserve the decorum of his estate; he reminds Usha of her 'lowly' origins and how she was 'rescued' by him; for good measure, he slaps her across the face. Humiliatingly for Usha, Dalvi must 'rescue' her; he shows up, eager for her to get to work and rescue his financial fortunes. Usha declines Dalvi's invitation to 'come home' and returns to her hotel. In the last scene, alone, she stares out of the window; fade to black, as we realize Usha has decided not to return to her older life, that she will move on alone from here.

Bhumika's bleak ending is optimistic in expressing Usha's attainment of the political and existential consciousness that her true happiness lies in independence from men, and indeed, from all familial structures, insofar as they are afflicted by patriarchy; the traditional life she has long dreamed of, under the influence of the patriarchal ideologies on which she was raised, cannot be hers. At home, Usha is exploited in one way; in the public, she is exploited in yet another. In neither sphere can she find a partner who will accept her unreservedly, as both an artist and a free woman worthy of respect; the forms of patriarchy change in the public and private, but its content and valence endures regardless.

Usha's sexual and romantic boldness, her moving on from partner to partner, her unwillingness to let herself be confined by the bounds of one relationship, though romantically unsatisfying, has a powerful existential implication: Usha would not have gained independence from men, had she not 'found out' whether such relationships worked, and to abandon them when they did not. She has paid a price for this experiential knowledge of her 'true self', but so do those, in far greater measure, who remain ignorantly confined in abusive, oppressive relationships. Usha's mother had cursed her to eternal unhappiness, a distinctively Indian mingling of the material and the supernatural that suggested a dark fate for a woman whose fate is controlled by supernatural forces; but the forces that directed Usha's life are earthly social and political realities that work to the advantage of those she lived her life with. Usha's final 'role', that of 'the lonely woman', is one her life's roles have best prepared her for; her prior life over as preparation, she is ready to play this one as we leave her.

Bhumika, like *Nishant*, offers a critique of the warped, toxic masculinity that results from patriarchy. Rajan, Usha's friendly co-worker, is a narcissist, unable to extend genuine commitment to Usha when she most needs it; the 'philosophical director' Sunil can only offer glib posturing, a species of vacuous philosophizing which is visibly inauthentic and superficial, unmoored from any connection with meaningful human relationships; Kale is comfortably ensconced in his feudal understanding of a woman's place, content to assert masculine force as and when needed to enforce its strictures (his former wife, well aware he is instantiating a patriarchal type, remarks, 'The beds change, the kitchens change. Men's masks change, but men don't change'); as for Dalvi, his only concessions to Usha's freedom and self-determination occur when he senses she might be driven away; his motivations for backing down, for 'acceptance', are to not compromise his source of income.

In *Bhumika* then, the men in Usha's life are two-dimensional and 'simple', confined to patriarchal roles, while Usha is complex, posing a puzzle for their sensibilities that they remain unable or unwilling to 'solve'. The men we see Usha with are products of patriarchal society where they are never tested or examined and remain mired in mediocrity; patriarchy is indicted for producing lesser, self-deluded men.[23] *Bhumika* concludes self-empowerment from such weaklings is realized by rejecting their fraught companionship in a sexist world; Usha's arrival at this awareness follows a long journey that began in her childhood when she noticed the limited choices available to her mother and grandmother, where she noticed the requirement of a man to rescue her from her home's dysfunction, a man whose early interactions with her set the stage for her later ones with all men. In Freudian terms, Usha found a replacement father in Keshav Dalvi; in *Bhumika* we witness her prolonged journey to grow out and away from the resultant oppressive paternal figure.

Benegal indicts Indian cinema as a crucial modality of the cultural oppression of Indian women; the men who interact with Usha require her to enact, even in the private, the roles she enacts in the public; they, like her, have been brought up on a steady diet of the particularly Indian cinematic depictions of women. If indeed, 'movies are constitutive of India's cultural being and determinative of its moral sensibility',[24] then Usha's lovers' ignorance of her needs is plausibly fuelled, in part at least, by the misrepresentations she has supplied to them, passionately and powerfully, via her roles on Indian screens. And she must, for that is the only way she may make a living, her life's choices determined by those of her mother and grandmother, and by a deluded man from whom she could only find relief through the company of equally deluded men.

Bhumika continues Benegal's critical notes as philosopher of culture in showing Usha is 'culturally oppressed', for she finds herself defined and understood by Indian masculinity and patriarchy's historically established images and understandings of women; but her desire to find requited love and respect for her craft offers active resistance to confirming such definitions. At home, as a child, Usha is fed rice but denied vegetables; this shocking scene, which depicts a physical deprivation common for rural Indian girls, brings the relationship between culture and justice to life, showing that in times of material scarcity, 'custom and political arrangements . . . decree who gets to eat the little there is'.[25] Instead, as Usha will find out, her worth to her family, 'her bargaining position', will be determined 'by her ability to work outside'. Crucially, Usha does not accept this treatment as a 'natural fact'; *Bhumika* persistently and powerfully articulates her persistent and continuing dissatisfaction with, and resistance to, the states of affairs dictated to her. The painful separation between patriarchal society's expectations and demands and Usha's relentless need for self-affirmation is *Bhumika*'s central moral and political statement.

Bhumika remains a landmark of feminist cinema, indeed, one of its purest expressions, an ambitious undertaking showcasing a cinephile's love of the movies, and a deep understanding of their political role in culture. It is visually dazzling and emotionally resonant in moving from black and white to colour to sepia, in capturing the dynamics of a spirited and independent life; we receive an education in cinema as well as sexual politics. The artistic collaboration between Benegal and his cinematographer Govind Nihalani finds particularly vivid expression here: cinema expresses the dynamic transitions of nations and their people; the separation between the artifice of the screen and the empirical reality of those who inhabit and sustain it allows for a deep and sensitive articulation of the split between the public and the private. The human drama on display finds new expression through the changing stocks of film; as cinema evolves and changes so does the life of those who sustain its images. If *Bhumika*'s central conclusions are bleak, it is, too, affirming and optimistic in suggesting that even within the most oppressive of worlds, women may contest patriarchy and find themselves on their own terms.

Mandi

Mandi (The Marketplace, 1983), inspired and informed by the Urdu short story *Anandi* by Ghulam Abbas, offers many cinematic and philosophical goods: a comic exploration of Indian sexuality centred on women; a mordant commentary on the relentless commercialization of India and its urban and rural spaces; an exposure of the hypocrisy, prudery and artifice of bourgeois society, which persists in 'othering' those which it calls on to satisfy its 'forbidden desires'; and 'a burlesque on politics and middle-class morals' valorizing unconventional 'survival' and 'freedom'.[26] The brothel and its prostitutes – the centrepieces of *Mandi* – steer clear of long-standing and clichéd tropes of 'golden-hearted prostitutes' (Hollywood's *Pretty Woman*) or the glamorous ghazal-singing, poetry-quoting *tawaifs* who perform for wealthy wine-drinking nawabs (the Indian film industry's *Umrao Jaan*). This unglamorous world is not romanticized; its grittiness is visible through its lusty and loud bawdiness, its ritzy dresses and adornments. The lusty women of the *mandi*, with their ample, exposed bosoms and midriffs, their loosely draped saris and tightly buttoned blouses bursting at the seams, are unapologetic about their unbridled sexuality, their risqué evocation of masculine desire; they are aware of the power their sexuality grants them in their boudoirs, which even if one lacking in public political valence is often able to reduce a man to a supplicant in private spaces.

At the *mandi*, all can be transacted; its clients are not dark-haired, handsome, moping, poets seeking a bottle of wine, a quiet haven and a sympathetic, intimate audience; rather, here may be found those who come seeking the gratification denied to them in 'respectable' society, which does not allow their sexuality full expression, or effaces it altogether. The realities of prostitute life remain grim, for the material pressures of the patriarchal world permit no sustained escape for its inhabitants. Neither does its hypocrisy; the *mandi* functions as a venue for escape from, as well as a scapegoat for, the varied moral ills of the society that surrounds it. The prostitutes' presence on the margins of society serves to remind those more fortunately placed of their social blessings, their not inconsiderable social privilege and capital, of the limits of respectability and the 'normal', and of the lives of those who are destined to not be judged so. Like the hijras (eunuchs) who are called on to bless a wedding or a newly born child in India, these 'outcastes', by their presence, sanctify the customs which marginalize them; they help define the boundaries of social propriety.

The brothel and the prostitute, and their paid sexual work, allow Benegal to rebuke society that its patriarchal conventional ordering and understanding of sexual morality and human sexual relations is skewed; for the prostitute both serves to disguise, and perpetuate and enable, a crippled and impoverished understanding of human sexuality. Rukmini Bai, the 'madam' of the brothel, proudly informs those who would condemn her, 'It is because of us that society functions. We alleviate social ills!' The 'social ill' in question remains unnamed, but we are tempted to surmise, based on the evidence, that it is unrequited sexuality, forced to find expression in unconventional venues, to find 'cover' in pretension and artifice and hypocrisy.

The *mandi*'s 'madam' is the matronly Rukmini Bai (Shabana Azmi) now past her best years, a complex character inviting identification and repulsion, wearing gaudy clothes and flashy jewellery and chewing betel leaves, struggling to keep the world at bay. As a 'madam', Rukmini is sophisticated enough to call in a doctor for periodic medical check-ups on her diverse, feisty 'wards'; she is not lacking in courage either, for when faced with an abusive customer, she haughtily throws him out, saying, 'This is Rukmini Bai's *kotha*, threaten someone else!' Rukmini has asserted control over her life, a measure of economic self-sufficiency, but she has done so on the backs of other women, and she remains at the mercy of larger cultural forces, unable to control her destiny adequately in the face of the patriarchal and commercial world's moral and material compulsions. In a dirge bemoaning the woman's lot she speaks of her hard life, drenched in mud and pushed hither and thither, betrayed by her one unidentified true love, leading her to freely tender the hard-learned wisdom of 'Never trust men, they are all crooks'. For Rukmini, woman is a kite, directionless and rudderless, moved along by external forces; but crucially, Rukmini has attempted to seize the controls through her stewardship of the *mandi*, asserting ownership and control of a material means of sustenance finely tuned to satisfying society's otherwise unexpressed 'needs'.

Rukmini Bai is, too, aware of the disapproving male gaze on her and knows what to do with it. In an early scene, the proverbial bystander of history, the jester, the brothel's drunken manservant Dungrus, rants and raves at night, invoking the Bai's 'bad deeds', the moral rot that, like termites, has set into the foundations of her home. He gloomily predicts that when she dies no one will lay her to rest; she has earned 'cursed money' and invoked the wrath of God for having sinned in exploiting women. Dungrus's anger at Rukmini Bai in this extended scene offers an explicit and extended articulation of the male disapproval of the *mandi*'s moral and legal sinners.[27] But this is a man's voice passing judgement, and Rukmini, roused from her slumbers by this loud disturbance, makes a simple but effective intervention, dismissing Dungrus and telling him to go to sleep. Her summary dismissal of the male gaze is an important allegory for her life – she is aware of it, but she is not cowed by it, and certainly she is only concerned to cater to those men who threaten her in material terms, and not just disapprove of her. Being a loud, disapproving man is not enough – those are a dime a dozen; you must be of the right class as well, one able to direct the contours of Rukmini's life. This is intersectional analysis too; as with Lakshmi in *Ankur*, Rukmini's demeanour with men varies depending on their location in the complex Indian matrix of caste, class and gender.

Benegal's materialist inclinations are visible in his claims that the *mandi* is equally at the mercy of commercial pressures and social sanctimony; its uncomfortably marginalized cultural position makes it vulnerable to both. The *mandi*'s new landlord, the businessman Gupta – symbolizing wealth, power and social respectability – regards it as a site for future commercial development, sparking a palpable contrast between the marginalized and those who hold the directing reigns of society. (In *Mandi*'s opening scene the efficient and unsentimental Gupta concludes a transaction to purchase land for commercial exploitation; we see the desiccated bones of an animal carcass as vultures gather; an older India and its culture have died, surrendering in the face of a rapacious and relentless commercialism.) The women, peripheral players in the new India, symbolize the faded, decadent glory of a house once frequented by nawabs; Gupta is the moneyed, unsophisticated, yet powerful, face of the new 'uncultured' India. Rukmini Bai must ingratiate herself with the new landlord and place herself and her women at his mercy as she bemoans the lack of appreciation for their work: 'We reduce daily loneliness and give the homeless comfort and shelter', and play a broader cultural role too; at a social gathering, when the women of the *mandi* sing classical ghazals, whose lyrics were composed by the erstwhile Mughal emperor, Bahadur Shah Zafar, Rukmini Bai suggests the modern Hindi film is a repository of degraded culture, of loud garish dances and pop music; it is her *mandi* and its women who maintain the classical arts. (This sly line continues a trend by Benegal of self-reflexive commentary on Indian cinema, whether the cinephile's homages of *Bhumika*, *Mammo* and *Suraj Ka Satwan Ghoda* or the critical, ironic notes struck here and in *Bhumika*.)

Benegal makes critical note in *Mandi* of the sexual marketing and exploitation of women that brothels rely on for their existence. For the *mandi*'s dark side is human trafficking; a young woman, Phoolmani, betrayed into sexual slavery by a pimp who has married her under false pretence, is its latest 'procurement'. Phoolmani is a deaf mute; but the men who will sleep with her desire her body; all else is irrelevant in the depersonalized space of the *mandi*'s sexual chambers. (A photographer who flirts with, and seeks to take risqué and nude photos of, the women of the *mandi*, which he may subsequently manipulate, points to the women's disposability and replaceability; he is society's voyeur, marketing and selling bodies. The photographer, too, represents and embodies patriarchal society's pornographic impulse, which treats these women's sexuality and bodies as anonymous, mass-produced consumer products.) The transactional conversation between Bai and the 'seller' refers to the young woman as a milch cow; we see women reduced to actively collaborating with men who traffic in their bodies. Rukmini's later expulsion of a customer who attacks Phoolmani is protectiveness of valuable, fungible property, not a person; any tenderness directed at her health is prudential concern over 'damaged goods' and 'industry reputation'. Phoolmani's tale thus generates an unpleasant, morally significant, contrast between the supposed artistic pretensions of Rukmini Bai and her brothel and the sordidness of Phoolmani's sexual abuse. (An overweight and lazy policeman, symbolizing the absent and uncaring state and its complicity in the exploitation of women, fails to detect the sexual trafficking being carried on right under his nose. Later, this policeman quotes legal absurdities when Phoolmani requires medical assistance. Insofar as the state is visible, it is present as either indifference, farcical irrelevance or active, damaging disruption.)

Phoolmani's tale allows Benegal to construct a morality play centring on the conflict between the *mandi* and its home in the surrounding town, for her plight soon attracts the attention of the humourless and haughty 'social worker' Shanti Devi, whose activist group, Nari Niketan (Women's Home), symbolizing the forces of conventional 'respectability', condemns the brothel, declaring their desire to 'protect' Indian culture and women. In response, Rukmini Bai points out, quite rightly, that men demand, and buy, what women sell; if Devi wishes to reform, she must start with men and their needs. This task is clearly intractable; it is the women who must give way, and so they are expelled from the city to a new site outside it. There, at the new *mandi*, the women find the local atmosphere hostile and their solidarity, even if asserted in self-defence, begins to fall apart in the face of rejection by their neighbours – here too, the women are accused of defilement, if not of social boundaries, then of actual sacredness, the site of an ancient temple. Dissension appears as the women revolt against Rukmini; the brothel disintegrates as the *mandi*'s members, their solidarity crumbling, make plans for a new life beyond it. Rukmini and Dungrus leave the *mandi*, her reign seemingly over, but a wild-eyed mystic intervenes, directing her to a chosen spot 'to find what you need'. On digging, Dungrus finds a *shivling*, a good omen, and Rukmini bows down, convinced her redemption is at hand. And indeed, she receives instant confirmation of her changed fortunes as we see a white sari-clad woman running towards the camera. It is Phoolmani, who has escaped from the 'shelter' of her 'home' with Shanti Devi's activist group; she runs towards the camera, towards Rukmini and the *mandi*, away from 'respectable society' and the 'shelter' it afforded. Phoolmani is the seed of the new *mandi*; Rukmini has a new 'daughter', a new home and a new life. Fade to black.

Mandi's feminism finds its grounding in the cultural marginalization directed at women who fulfil a vital, if hidden, social 'role' whose societal burdens and costs must be borne only by them. Patriarchy's notions of female sexuality, its artificial dichotomies and harsh moralizing, creates the Madonna–Whore divide; the prostitute is the social creature who fulfils the need created by the resultant compromised sexuality – even as she herself must remain marginalized and condemned. Rukmini Bai is the foster mother for an ostensibly 'respectable' businessman's love child through a former member of the *mandi*, who cannot be recognized on pain of social shame, and she fights to keep that young woman 'respectable', a virgin committed to the arts, an artist of distinction whom the world will otherwise regard as a mere whore. But the Bai cannot raise her head to be acknowledged by society for her private 'work' of child rearing (or, for that matter, her public work of the maintenance and propagation of the classical arts). Benegal thus offers a brilliant subversion of the social valorization of traditional parenting: Bai's motherhood is an unacknowledged aspect of her personality and 'social labour' for whatever society considers her to be, it is not a mother; motherhood's 'respectable' standing, a vital cultural good that would serve as the foundation for valuable social capital, is to be denied her because she is the owner of a brothel. But this 'whore' is a better parent than the 'respectable' businessman who, not finding sexual satisfaction at home – perhaps because of his wife's repressed and policed sexuality – impregnated a prostitute but disowned the child that resulted from that liaison. Like Usha in *Bhumika*, the women of the *mandi* enjoy a curious freedom within their cage; unrestrained within, they may not enjoy traditional motherhood or the household, or indeed, any sort of public approval from larger society; these fruits are denied to them. More broadly, conventional culture cannot find a place for them in its honour roll of 'artists', even as it exploits their labour in their pursuit of the classical arts, which are reinvigorated by their presence and practice.

The women in *mandi* are economically marginalized, too, because they cannot find a living in the 'labour markets' of the world 'outside'. There they will be powerless, unable to 'participate in making decisions that affect the conditions of their lives'.[28] The women in *mandi* may work, but they are not recognized as workers; their work constructs 'value' which cannot be recognized or recompensed; they function as hidden labour, part of public society's 'private foundations', which sustain it without promise of recompense, whether material or theoretical. Some costs of this arrangement are uniquely theirs for they bear the brunt of social failure: a young woman is denied her identity, her mother's love, because of her father's cowardice, and elsewhere, kidnapped deaf-mute women find markets for sexual wares waiting for them. The material pressures on the *mandi* ensure it can never find a stable home; there is always a social altar on which the *mandi* and its women will be sacrificed, for their offerings are never sufficiently recognized in any social or cultural dimension. They remain as visible markers of the social pathology which has created them, and for which they continue to function as scapegoats.

Mandi prominently allows Benegal to explore female friendship and solidarity and women's collective resistance in facing society, a focus which makes it a 'hymn to the power and survival of woman'.[29] (A theme vividly present in *Mammo* and *Junoon* as well.) The solidarity and companionship of the brothel's residents are shown in group shots carefully constructed to display physical and psychic solidarity; the women huddle together, clasp each other's hands, rest their heads on each other's shoulders. We see sisterhood among women, brought together by the world that has rejected them; these women may squabble among themselves, but they will rise collectively to face an external threat, and they will not hesitate to come to another's aid. Within the confines of the brothel, its spaces, the women's relationships show passion, affection and friendship take many forms; their often-fierce internal conflicts show them to be not 'generic women' but humans with diverse inclinations, disagreements and contestations. The women in *Mandi* show that their 'Otherness' and their resultant different life experiences lead to a distinctive interpretive relationship with the world; they must develop their own culture, in their own spaces, with its own moral orderings and hierarchies. Within the walls of the brothel, the prostitutes construct a new home for themselves with new familial allegiances, commitments and duties. There is no talk of their erstwhile family or community; perhaps these women made their way to Rukmini's brothel after they were kidnapped, forced out of their homes, abandoned or fled an abusive husband or father who beat or raped them. The *mandi* is not just a place to conduct business; it is refuge too; as Phoolmani discovered, more so than Nari Niketan, her new 'shelter' and 'home'.

There is considerable ethical ambiguity in *Mandi*; we want to support Bai and her women but are appalled by that human trafficking which brought those women to Bai's 'home', and which is enabled by the Bai. We despise sanctimonious women like Shanti Devi but not her work and its professed political stance; we despise instead its lack of sympathy for those who should be, in at least one dimension, Devi's 'fellow travellers'. By provoking an inversion of 'conventional' sympathies, by 'supporting' the woman who supports the trafficking of a deaf-mute woman, by condemning ostensible symbols of respectability like the businessman, the arranged marriage and the social worker, we are led to suspect apparent societal respectability masks far greater pathologies. This ambiguity, and its resultant political ambivalence, demonstrate the identities and 'locations' of political actors are as important as the political ideologies sustained and conveyed by them; it matters who speaks, who acts and how; *Mandi* is thus an acute document of political realism.

In *Mandi* Benegal articulates, powerfully, the subversive notion that because of her unsentimental commodification of sex, the prostitute is the only genuinely 'free' woman in Indian society, one not dependent on the largesse of men; instead, in a culture of repressed sexuality, men are dependent on her for 'release' and 'expression'. The prostitute may thus be 'better off' than the Indian wife for the prostitute can command a price for her sexual labour; she can set times and hours for sexual access to her body outside the constraints of patriarchal expectations. Benegal's ironic script and narrative in *Mandi* allows for a deeply subversive point: We are tempted to condemn the sexual trafficking of women and the associated 'sex work', but how different is traditional marriage, Indian or otherwise, when its economic and sexual contractual terms are made transparent? The businessman Agrawal, a former patron of the *mandi*, has a transactional relationship with the bustling and entrepreneurial Gupta, whose daughter he has arranged for his son, Sushil, to marry to restore his finances. At the engagement party of Agrawal's son Sushil, Gupta's daughter is brought down to be displayed and married off; this is respectable society, but here, too, men inspect women for sexual compatibility and desirability. This alternative form of trafficking of women openly takes place in 'respectable' society and receives its formal blessings and approval – while the *mandi*'s prostitutes are present to sing songs serenading the manufactured love put on display. The simpering giggling of Gupta's daughter indicates she is too immature to be married, and yet she will be, to a man who will not allow her incomprehension of sex to get in his way of using her. How different then is Gupta's daughter, really, from Phoolmani, whom we recognize as a rape victim? The true *mandi* – Benegal's central thesis in *Mandi* – is patriarchal society itself.

Mandi artfully captures the opposition set up between women by patriarchy.[30] It is a woman, Shanti Devi, whose vocal, organized, systematic condemnation most threatens Rukmini in material terms. Shanti Devi's hypocrisy and hostility to the *mandi* is plausibly understood as a species of Freudian reaction formation; she lashes out at Rukmini and her workers, for they openly express a sexuality she cannot – as her illicit liaison with her son-in-law suggests. In her brief for the expulsion of the brothel from the city, Shanti Devi says she will not allow 'decency' to be sacrificed; the Municipal Corporation agrees there is no place in the city for Bai and 'women like her'. At their protest rally Devi's demonstrators claim that 'women should be worshipped', but when asked how they should be treated instead, can only answer that 'women should not be sold'. The women demonstrators claim they will 'talk to their sisters and demand they leave this work', but their 'sisters' at the *mandi* are scornful: 'How will we eat then?' When told 'eating is not everything', they retort, 'You must get it for free then.' This little exchange is a stronger argument for a materialist feminism than many pages of theoretical tracts; the gap between those who would impose a facile, 'liberal' moralizing on those who need material deliverance instead is exposed as wide and deep. So strong is Shanti Devi's prejudice against the women she wishes to 'help', so great her distance from their lives, that she declines their polite offering of the ceremonial *prasad* from the local temple; apparently, their mortal, earthly sins can taint even sacral offerings blessed by the gods.

The woman Shanti Devi 'rescues', Phoolmani, finds her new home at Shanti Niketan unbearable and flees – as she had tried to escape the *mandi* earlier. And she does so to return to her 'home', where, even if she had been abused, she had found some comfort in the company of women whose life experiences bore important similarities to hers. Benegal raises a disconcerting possibility: if marriage is socialized sexual slavery and labour exploitation, then perhaps Phoolmani is better off in a brothel, where she will find the friendship and warmth of other women, and be spared sanctimonious, patriarchal lectures on how to be a 'good mother' and 'good wife'. In the conventional home, too, Phoolmani would have to grit her teeth while men were permitted to construct pedestals for themselves of social propriety and demand her sexual 'services' for little to no material or emotional reward; those same men were exposed in the brothel as men desperately craving an unconventional sexual fix, their dignity momentarily held in abeyance while they forked over payments for sexual favours. Shanti Devi had asserted Phoolmani was not of a 'good character' as she kept wanting to escape; ironically, the runaway has found the faux sincerity of her 'shelter' unbearable and prefers her older 'home' where she found greater solidarity and companionship of the right kind.

The persistent hostility and mutual incomprehension that characterizes Rukmini Bai and Shanti Devi's relationship shows class separates these women: their differing life experiences ensure they do not see each other as 'comrades'. Indian middle-class women, who 'invite' poor women from neighbouring slums, displaced from their villages into the cities seeking work, into their homes as sweepers, dhobis and dishwashers, lack an understanding of the material and economic compulsions that make them so adept at bearing the burdens of others' lives. They, and high-caste Indian women, will enforce the strictures of a casteist and classist society as strictly as high-caste or upper-class men. Unsurprisingly, the self-professed 'global' female 'reformer' and 'liberator of women' Shanti Devi offers uncaring, unsympathetic opposition to a woman making an unconventional path for herself; the reformer's opposition is a problematic internalization of the same prejudices that have marginalized women – all of them, not just Rukmini and her wards. Rukmini Bai's supposed woman comrade and she are unable to communicate across the divide of caste and economic standing and indeed, their life experiences; here, there is no female solidarity to be seen. This depiction of Shanti Devi complicates the question of women's identity in a patriarchal world: in her political stance, Devi is as 'male' as any of the men who condemn Rukmini to disguise their own pathologies. Benegal suggests again, here, that gender is an especially contested notion when it is so impacted by the material hierarchies and arrangements that influence Rukmini Bai's and Shanti Devi's lives.

Mandi's closing claims Phoolmani might have found the hypocrisy of Nari Niketan's 'shelter' unbearable; there, too, she found traditional roles and expectations awaiting her, the best outcome for her a marriage to a man who would 'accept' her into a traditional household and subject her to familiar patriarchal pressures of providing sexual services and household work. From such a vantage position, one in which the truth of the proposition that marriage in a patriarchal society is not a medal but a sentence would have been evident to her, Phoolmani might have found the brothel a freer place, one where her sexual slavery would be the same, but her servitude to her client would end when he would walk out the door, a sobering thought for those who imagine acceptance by respectable society and its institutions remains the greatest prize of all.

Mammo

Muslim women in India who resist patriarchy, in whatever fashion, find themselves in a political bind. Indian liberals and feminists often consider them insufficiently emancipated, too tempted by reactionary and conservative Muslim religiosity, too resistant to a 'normal' religiosity and a 'liberated' liberalism defined in majoritarian, Hindu terms. Indian Muslims, conversely, consider them dangerously liberated, too keen to shake off their 'Muslim origins' and mingle in the Indian Hindu mainstream and take on 'subversive' or 'non-Islamic' values.[31] This resistance to a 'universalism' that refuses to recognize the particulars of Muslim women's lives, through an unexamined focus on middle-class, high-caste Hindus or on a narrowly understood and patriarchal notion of 'Muslim woman', suggests the theoretical and practical need for an intersectional Muslim feminism.[32]

Benegal's movies about Muslim women represent a significant contribution to this task: offering a sensitive exploration of the public and private lives of Indian Muslim women, they were produced in the 1990s, a decade that finds its political prominence in signalling the rise to power of the chauvinist Hindu nationalist party the Bharatiya Janata Party (BJP), which began the decade as a marginal political player and by its end was manoeuvring to seize central political power, a threat realized in the new millennium. The 1990s therefore marked a period of rising religious intolerance and polarization, egged on by a Hindu nationalism eager to settle old scores left over from the Partition of 1947. Hindu chauvinists found easy targets in the provision of a separate civil code for Muslims, rising Muslim separatism in Kashmir, and the continued hostility and intransigence of India's neighbour Pakistan. In the broader Indian culture, two television serials based on the great Indian epics, the *Mahabharata* and the *Ramayana*, were produced and broadcast weekly as a communitarian viewing exercise, turning them into giant public affirmations of India's allegedly 'Hindu nature'. In this charged political and cultural context, Muslims were easily regarded as fifth columnists and traitors, a foreign presence in the Indian polity that undermined its 'true, Hindu' cultural and moral leanings and inclinations. Benegal's movies on Muslim women reminded Indian viewers that Indian Muslims were Indians, that Muslim culture was a component of Indian culture, that Muslim women deserved liberation not just from Muslim patriarchy but from Hindu patronization and Indian patriarchy and narrow visions of the Indian nation too. Benegal's movies on Muslim women make their intersectional claims by making the location of Muslim women in Indian social hierarchies and arrangements *visible*, by reminding Indian women that their cohort included Muslim women who were like them, and yet faced unique challenges all their own. This set of movies – *Zubeidaa*, *Mammo* and *Sardari Begum* – is often described as a 'trilogy' for its running storyline of the family of Riyaz, a writer, and his mother, Zubeidaa, grandmother, Fayazi, and grandaunt Mahmuda Begum (Mammo); of these, I consider *Mammo* for the purposes of the present study.

Mammo (1994) allies itself with that species of postcolonial feminism which addressed women's place in 'postcolonial nation-building' and their 'problematic relationship to the state'.[33] It responds to that ever-growing body of literature which explores the trauma of lives sundered and reconfigured by the postcolonial forces of violent displacement set loose during the momentous days of the liberation of the Indian subcontinent from colonialism.[34] Indian women experienced 1947's Great Partition of the Indian subcontinent – which produced the nations of India and East and West Pakistan – differently depending on their caste, class and religion; and though families moved, inheritances were disposed, ties torn asunder, colonialism defeated, new nations created and princely states made subservient to democracy, patriarchy in its diverse forms – Indian, Pakistani, Hindu, Muslim – endured through it all. Muslim women, like Sikh and Hindu ones, suffered changes to their physical and psychic locations that were acutely tuned to their stations in their lives; within these changes such women, as *Mammo* makes clear, were often left to devise new lives for themselves.

In *Mammo*, the struggles of a new nation to find itself a new postcolonial form are mirrored in those of a woman, Mammo, who is engaged in similar contestation outside the patriarchal cloisters of her husband's home; she struggles for her personal freedom and self-realization as a pair of new nations struggle with the precise nature and dimensions of their newly acquired independence from colonial rule. Mammo's life, at the nexus of these larger political forces, finds itself determined by them; her struggle to find an emotional and tangible home within their interplay is *Mammo*'s central statement, a moving indictment of patriarchy and a nationalism, which obsessed with theoretical utopian visions, disdains the actual, realized fates of its intended citizens.

These contrasts, again between the public and the private, and the interplay of public forces pressing upon the private and those of the private driving public changes, allow Benegal to explore those narratives which enrich, conflict with, and help sustain or undermine the supposed facts of an 'official national history'. Benegal suggests this notion be replaced instead with that of 'national histories', each revealing a contestation not visible in the sanitized and denatured official version produced for the promulgation of national ideologies and the sustenance of nations; the 'official history' treats citizens as anonymous ciphers, reduced easily to statistical regularities. It is the unofficial, local, personal history that reveals the truly contingent, seething dynamic nature of the ever-changing entity called 'India'. In this context, to privilege the voice of a woman, and a Muslim one at that, is to make the claim that the nation's story is the story of *all* its citizens regardless of caste, class, gender or religion – a tangible statement of its egalitarian, secular, democratic aspirations and claims. The average Indian citizen remembers the 'freedom struggle' in unqualified fashion as a cavalcade of luminaries and an unambiguous subscription to the idea of the Indian nation; the actual history of post-independent India is of a dynamic, contested polity, which featured both large and small political struggles between political actors often opposed to each other. Low-caste Indians wondered whether colonial rule would simply be replaced by high-caste hegemony; the working classes speculated about the nature of their rights working for a newly empowered landowning and business class, and the women of India speculated whether the new extravagant language of self-determination and nationalist autonomy professed by India's 'freedom fighters' applied to them as much as it did to male Indians.

The Indian subcontinent's Muslims, for their part, found their identity problematized through the demands of Indian and Pakistani citizenship and nationalist commitment and the humiliations of 'loyalty oaths' in India – even as Muslim families were subject to the traumas of physical and political separation by Partition. Within this new national dispensation would the older identities of Muslims, men and women alike, be cast aside for those devised by the ambitious creators of new polities and nations? During the Partition, Muslim women transitioned from the patriarchy of nation and social context to that of another, finding no relief. From the feminist perspective this was not cause for surprise; the great uniter across time, space, cultures and religion, across the transformations from colonialism to postcolonialism, from parents' homes to those of in-laws, from Muslim families to Hindu families, is the domination, subordination and oppression of women by men in all walks of life.

Mammo, starring Farida Jalal, Surekha Sikri and Rajit Kapur, shows how a disempowered woman, an archetypal refugee dispossessed by larger political forces, finds the fruits of a modern liberal state, citizenship in a pluralistic democracy, denied her because her life's trajectories were determined by a patriarchy – whether Hindu or Muslim, Indian or Pakistani – which effaced her personal and political agency. The traditional history of postcolonial nations appears as a parade of dominant personalities and ideologies, of competitions between empires and nascent nations, between competing frameworks of politics. Benegal's lenses, which focus on the private, reveal that history is far more complicated as struggles and contestations between public political forces find dramatic and painful expression within the confines of single lives. In this cinematic miniature centring on two sisters separated by the Partition, Benegal concentrates on macro-political crises' micro-personal effects; he shows the political, moral and social tragedy of the Partition, a fantastically complex interaction of peoples and materials, was built on the foundation of innumerable minor personal ones. Within the cauldron of the Partition, older political priorities and orderings and hierarchies asserted themselves and found new and distinctive expression in the lives of political subjects. Refugee men and women lost their lives and homes; the women were dispossessed or forced to move by those who directed their agency, or treated as chattel, disposable items of property. Too often, women found themselves caught between contesting nationalisms and paid a price not accounted for in the historical reckonings of the Partition's human and material tolls. Mammo (Mahmuda Begum), the titular character in *Mammo*, is a refugee, one of the Partition's many casualties, her life's trajectories determined by her identity as a Muslim woman – one understood differently in the two nascent nations, India and Pakistan, she might consider her homes. Her experiences show 'the scripts of Nation and Nationalism have serious effects' for women, especially if 'Nation and Nationalism' have not taken women on board in their theoretical and practical visions.[35]

Mammo offers a sympathetic, intimate examination of the lives of Mammo and Fayazi, who unite around the upbringing of their grandson and grandnephew Riyaz in the financially fraught environment of the big city; they are hemmed in by the destitution that threatens them on the dissolution of their family. (The two sisters are on their own, for their third sister and her husband have sold off their old home and kept the proceeds, condemning the two to a modest, hardscrabble life.) Fayazi is committed to raising Riyaz by herself after his abandonment by his uncaring father, who remarried all too soon once his actress mother, Zubeidaa, Fayazi's daughter, had passed away.[36] Mammo, who was made an outsider in her own land, a 'foreigner' and a 'traitor' for Indians, by her father's decision to migrate to Pakistan after Partition and marry her off to a Pakistani man, joins Fayazi and Riyaz in Mumbai after she is widowed. She has been made a traitor and a refugee again by her Pakistani in-laws' mistreatment of her after her husband's death, by the discrimination tendered her in Pakistan because she was an 'outsider', even though Muslim, from India. Mahmuda Begum is a victim of history and circumstance and patriarchy; the troubles she details with her in-laws – the loss of independence and respectable status within the household following the death of her husband – are familiar to Indian women, but their expression as a transnational crisis is due to the intersections of postcolonial politics in her life. Women lose homes when they marry, but Mammo's loss of home is twofold, for she loses India and Pakistan in turn thanks to patriarchal pressures. Now, India cannot welcome her, insisting on a new identity and not letting her enjoy the older one she never gave up voluntarily. If there is a home for her in this new world, it is in the private, with her family.

Mammo's life and that of his grandmother are visible to the young Riyaz, who acquires from them a sympathetic and empathetic understanding of his caretakers and thus a deeper appreciation of human grace under pressure, an acute sensitivity for a budding writer to acquire; Mammo and Fayazi might not know it, but they have given ink to this writer's pen. Their interactions with Riyaz show us a writer in the making as a synthesis of an inquiring intelligent mind with emotionally resonant experiences. His moral instructors in this education are two women, Mammo and Fayazi, who turn out to be the mother and friend the missing Zubeidaa could have been.

In *Mammo*'s melancholic opening scene, one underwritten powerfully by a plaintive ghazal sung by Jagjit Singh (a noted Indian exponent of classical vocal music), Riyaz wakes and sits down to write; in another room Fayazi performs her morning namaaz. He asks her where her sister, his 'Mammo Nani (grandmother)', now absent, but acutely missed, is; Riyaz's mention of Mammo's absence is cause for Fayazi to be stricken by guilt at not having responded more volubly and affectionately to her many letters from Pakistan asking for help and shelter. As the young man reads her letters from the past, pleading to be called back home, away from her oppressive domestic situation, we flashback to a knock on the door, to a time when Riyaz was a mere boy, to Mammo's previous return to India from Pakistan, where she had been taken – like other Indian Muslim women who 'migrated' to the new nation – after the Partition of India by her father. That first move had lacked agency, this surprise return to India does not. Now, she has fled 'back home', complaining of her mistreatment by her in-laws in Pakistan, for the day 'he' died, all went wrong. Now she has asserted agency, she has been decisive, she has not stayed on to bear her fate. Despite finding Lahore a more salubrious city, she considers this city, Mumbai, her own land, and has come 'home', back to her sister and her grandnephew.

The callow Riyaz is initially intolerant of Mammo's presence but is forced to reconcile himself to her enforced presence in his personal life. Uncomfortable with her lack of cultural sophistication, conscious of his status as an 'orphan' of a modest background among his middle-class, Anglophone public school mates, Riyaz lies about his grandaunt to his school mates but slowly develops a loving and caring relationship with her. Mammo, for her part, strives to build ties with her difficult nephew, a 'perfect stranger', a task facilitated by her defences of Riyaz through his many boyish escapades, like watching movies like *Psycho* while cutting class, the scenes of which segment amount to another homage to the movies from Benegal, and his perusal of the risqué pleasures of *Playboy*. They bond, too, over his precocious love for the movies as they watch M. S. Sathyu's 1973 classic of 'partition cinema' *Garam Hawa* – allowing Benegal to unify their experiences as post-partition Indian Muslims with those of the unfortunate fictional Mirza family – and his ambitions to be a writer, fuelled by his curiosity about Mammo's life, his desire to live with 'lots of experiences so I can write about them' even as Mammo, scarred and traumatized by the murderous Partition, replies, 'There are some things you should not experience, like seeing hell in this life.' Mammo thus becomes a messenger from a distant time and land, conveying news to Riyaz about the political and moral fractures that have resulted in the nation of which he is now a citizen.

Mammo, an outsider in her older home and newer homes, between sundered communities and polities, finds a home with Fayazi and Riyaz, which may provide succour and solace, but her desires for safe domesticity are not congruent with the political realities of two new nations. She applies for an extension to her Indian visa but is undone by a combination of human greed and implacable governmentality; the Indian police arrive with a deportation order and duly enforce it by dragging her away – from her 'real home' – to put her on a 'train to Pakistan', back to her 'official' political home where she can find no welcome or caring like the familial one she can in her 'unofficial' home. At the end of *Mammo*, which is shot in one long flashback, Mammo returns to Fayazi's door again. She asserts to the overjoyed and disbelieving Riyaz and Fayazi that she will not return to Pakistan, relying on a fake death certificate asserting she died in India, turning her into a spirit, an ephemeral *chirag ka jinn*, not a real, tangible person. Indeed, as far as the nations of India and Pakistan are concerned, Mammo has never been a real person with a voice and independent desire but always a mere cipher, an abstract 'Muslim woman' or 'Pakistani illegal alien'. It is only with her sister and her grandnephew, within the private, that she finds her public self affirmed.

In *Mammo* women find survival and flourishing in the company of other women, on their own; the company and approval of men is neither available nor required; the men who have dictated Mammo and Fayazi's life's fortunes are absent or uncaring. This 'kinship of women' is explored through Mammo and Fayazi's intimate relationship which provides emotional and material sustenance to them, and whose interactions – affectionate, irritable and cranky – show 'sisterhood' being worked through as the two sisters collectively resist cultural, material and economic forces that oppress them. The sisters often squabble with great passion and vehemence but make up with expressions of regret and affection, an emotional resilience which is an indispensable tool of survival for women who rely on finding companionship, solace and sustenance in each other. Still, even as Fayazi keeps up a constant refrain of her sad lot – the weekday drudgery, the limited and unreliable income, the absence of a caring life partner, the slim prospects of economic or personal relief – she continues to function efficiently and lovingly as parent, grandmother and moral guardian. Mammo and Fayazi's common burden of widowhood – abandoned by family and made destitute, left to care for a boy deserted by his absent, callous and uncaring father – establishes a bond with other Indian women: they fear the loneliness and destitution forced on them by society, and not the mere physical infirmity of their old age. Mammo and Fayazi maintain a dignified front, a stoic facing up to the world; Mammo is defiant, unwilling to accept the pittance of the handout given by the third sister as an attempt to buy their compliance; Fayazi is utterly dedicated to the caretaking of her spirited and intelligent grandson.

Women find solidarity across religious boundaries, too, and unite in resistance to patriarchy: after Shanta, the Hindu maidservant of Fayazi's household, is abused and assaulted at home, Mammo accosts the drunk husband in his lair, slaps him and tells him to seek forgiveness from his wife. In this scene, there is no shirking by Mammo of her 'sisterly duty' on grounds of religious difference or national identity; she unquestioningly rises to the defence of a woman whose plight she empathizes with. The sisterhood on display here is like that of *Mandi* in an important sense: women find true companionship only when they are with other women. Sometimes even with those of other religions and castes and classes; if intersectional feminism bids us explore the multiple axes of oppression in a women's life, it instructs us, too, on how women from different socio-economic strata can form alliances against their common foe: patriarchy.

Mammo's life and her distinct experiences speak to the need for diverse feminisms. A narrower feminism would not consider her sufficiently 'liberated'; she does not, after all, seek out a wholly new identity divorced from her older, family-and-religion-based identity, casting off the burkha and an oppressive, patriarchal, religious tradition to seek out remarriage and sexual and economic liberation. There is, too, in Mammo, no visible or overt defiance of conservative Islamic strictures: Mammo wears a full body burkha when she goes out of the house; she teaches Qur'an classes; her speech is peppered with allusions to Allah and to verses of the Qur'an. Both sisters diligently and seriously offer their daily namaaz; they do not rebel against Islam or religious traditions. But their religious observances do not oppress the two sisters as much as do the political machinations of nationalism and patriarchy. It was not political Islamism or religious fundamentalism that made Mammo move to Pakistan as much as her father's will, one that did not incorporate her desires into its complex reckonings; it is not Islam that beckoned her back to India for she left a Muslim nation for a secular one. To Hindu Indians, Mammo, by virtue of her migration to Pakistan, has betrayed India, not shown the appropriate allegiance; to Pakistani Muslims, Mammo has betrayed the Islamic ideals of Pakistan to return to the secular state of India. But nowhere are Mammo and Fayazi oppressed by private religious faith as much as they are by religious faith made into a spearhead for nationalism. Mammo's return to India does not so much as betoken a preference for the Indian state, for a secular mode of life, in preference to an Islamic one, as much as it is a powerful statement of familial affection and commitment; her relationship with Fayazi offers powerful testimony to the claims of family and friendship over those of nation and religion. A feminism or nationalism which asked

Mammo to sacrifice her family for a larger political cause would find an unwilling political ally here.

In *Mammo*, an *ethics of care* brings value and meaning to its character's lives; each individual, autonomous assertion of independence by its women characters is bounded and determined by others' needs.[37] Fayazi's life is defined by the responsibility she takes for raising her grandson, by finding meaning through 'interdependence and care'.[38] Mammo leaves her in-laws' home but only to seek out her sister and grandson; she does not seek out life on her own. Neither Fayazi nor her seek to free themselves from familial bonds; they seek only to exchange one kind of bond for another. In Benegal's cinema, women are always enmeshed in a rich web of relationships; his women characters do not strive for a totalizing independence because they 'perceive and construe social reality . . . around experiences of attachment and separation'.[39] Fayazi and Mammo 'realize' themselves via caring, not via isolation from the interests of others; the two sisters have not 'wasted' their lives; they have made them considerably richer. The relationships of Fayazi and Mammo, with each other and their grandnephew and grandson, make us notice that fictional 'contracts between freely consenting, wholly autonomous, adults' are not 'the paradigm source of moral obligation'; rather it is *maternal virtue*, which provides children their first experiences of justice, and ensures 'new humans' are 'made appropriately welcome and prepared for their adult lives'.[40] Attentiveness, responsibility, competence and responsiveness underwrite the ethics of care Mammo and Fayazi embody; but in taking care of others, women often do not take care of themselves and remain inattentive to their own needs, an inattention that may provoke rage and self-destructiveness. Both Mammo and Fayazi are infected by such anger; the miracle we witness is they are not consumed by it. Their salvation can be found in their companionship and their love for each other and their ward, Riyaz.

In Fayazi's family and its workings, Benegal shows how an ethics of care facilitates the moral and intellectual development of its wards. As a minor miracle, Fayazi has raised an inquisitive young boy who attends an English public school, who despite his Muslim identity and insecure economic status – one not fully established with his classmates – is integrated into mainstream society. These are significant achievements for Fayazi, a Muslim widow subject to social discrimination for lacking a male partner, and to economic discrimination for lacking marketable skills denied her because of her exclusion from traditional labour markets. Riyaz's growth to accept Mammo after his initial impatience, his growing sensitivity as a person, is marked by his recognition of the maternal care she and his grandmother have brought to his life; his maturity in the personal and artistic realms is marked by his growing understanding of how his claims to his distinctive talent and individuality have been facilitated by his upbringing by these women; his recognition of Mammo's caring for him proceeds from, and is facilitated by, a long-awaited recognition and acceptance of his grandmother. Riyaz could have grown up to be a chauvinist like his absent father; instead, he has been 'forged' in a woman's home into a sensitive and creative writer. Miraculously, Riyaz has escaped the worst of patriarchy, because he was brought up by a pair of women in the absence of a father, a sobering thought for those men who wonder wherein the arc of their moral improvement lies.

3

'Bringing stories to life'
The storyteller

The titular trope above suggests literary works lie dormant and desiccated, awaiting revival by the movie, but some literary works 'die' on the screen, the writerly flair and the moral and aesthetic vision of the novelist eradicated by a deadpan literal transfer of text to celluloid (or digital frame). Benegal's 'literary movies', his cinematic reworkings of minor and major works of literature, produce new, 'vital' interpretations – which show how the 'original work' captured the universal in the particular – by way of passage to the screen. Benegal's 'literary movies' spring from diverse Indian languages and traditions; here we find Anglo-Indian, Hindi and Marathi novels; the greatest epic of all – the *Mahabharata* and an original screenplay. This diversity of literary forms, styles and concerns is marked by a thematic unity: each work instantiates and provokes fundamental political, ethical and metaphysical commentary. Within them, a broad array of themes of Benegal's work persist, endure and find new expression and embodiment: women's sexuality; caste and class divisions and conflict; patriarchal oppression; colonialism, anti-colonialism and postcolonialism's private; the philosophy of literature and fiction; nationalism and identity; the nature of religious belief; the varieties of 'truths'; alternative epistemologies; the relationship between religion and rebellion; the cultural and psychological reproduction of moral and historical archetypes across time and space; the nature of obsessional love; the nature of time and memory and remembrance and forgetting; and ultimately, the construction of selves, national and personal.

In each movie under consideration here, Benegal coaxes from the original literary 'raw material', a cinematic version that is not a faithful visual transcription of the text, but rather, a theoretically and artistically productive reimagining of the impulses that underwrote the original text's forays into the philosophical; there is considerable cinematic indulgence here but always at the service of an acute moral and political vision. In so far as Benegal's cinema permits experimentation with conventional texts, it is constrained by the artistic norms that avant-garde cinematic translations and interpretation of texts are self-indulgent exercises in sterile aestheticism if they lack such inspiration, and that literature neither demands nor requires a banal visual transcription. The work that results from the encounter of literature with its cinematic counterparts must be a 'new work'; as Vladimir Nabokov noted in writing of translations, the demand for 'fidelity to the original' is incoherent for they should include as much of the translator and the translated as they must of the original. Benegal's movies are such new works; they bring their 'source' with them, but strike out beyond it, there to claim new domains of meaning and understanding. The cinematic translations Benegal provides here are, like his other works, multimodal: stories acquire vocal and instrumental, classical and modern, soundtracks and physical landscapes; fictional characters acquire corporeal manifestation and voices with timbre and pitch; places and settings acquire physical locations, the imagined world of the word takes shape. From this assemblage of the spoken, the heard, the seen, the felt emerges a unique cultural production: the Indian literary movie – here, enduring philosophical theses are brought forth, to find newer expression and valence.

Junoon

The Anglo-Indian writer Ruskin Bond's novel *A Flight of Pigeons*, set at the time of the East India Company's colonial rule over India and the Indian Mutiny of 1857, is a literary work with no apparent philosophical pretensions. *Junoon* (Obsession, 1978), Benegal's cinematic interpretation of Bond's novel, offers an acute commentary on colonialism and gender relations in its exploration of sexuality, love and obsession which spans the colonial public and private. The political, cultural and religious dynamics of Indian resistance to colonialism are placed at *Junoon*'s margins to centre the private drama at play; Benegal's direction is not oversight but deliberate emphasis. The public details of the Indian Mutiny of 1857 are the subject of extensive historiography; an alternative 'modern Indian history' – of which academic history, and popular and art house cinema are significant components – seeks to bring the hidden private, the 'story of the masses', to light as well. In this dimension, *Junoon* offers a sharp examination of private aspects of the public phenomena of modern Indian history: friendships, informal allegiances, personal relationships, family ties, all to be found in the home and hearth. *Junoon*'s larger poetic and moral commitment is to the redeeming power of love and the complications of sexual obsession, its untrammelled force in the face of ideology, nationalism and colonialism; in the private cloister, love flourishes amid personal contestations, while war between the forces of colonialism and a budding nationalism, and bloody, ruthless reprisal, rages in the world outside.

The central issue in *Junoon* is a dispute over the possession of a woman's body: a white Christian mother, Mariam Labadoor, overcome by a colonial racial and religious panic, defends her daughter, Ruth Labadoor, against the threatening 'dark forces' of the colonial subcontinent, personalized in a brown heathen man, a brooding Muslim Pathan, Javed Khan. Khan is wholly infatuated with Ruth, but seeks to possess her not by sexual assault but by marriage and 'respectable' customs; another woman, Khan's wife, Firdaus, resists this encroachment, this violation of her personal privilege, on her private domain. The patriarchal public and his masculine pretensions allow the Pathan to assert force in seizing the Labadoor family after the outbreak of the Mutiny's violence, and in keeping them as prisoners; the colonial private in the form of Mariam, and all that stands behind her, exerts its own counterforce, restraining him from seizing his patriarchal and masculine dues in the body of Ruth. This private battle between Mariam and Javed is matched in parallel with the larger forces of the public as Indian rebels wage war against colonial armies and their collaborators on battlefields away from the homes that house their women.

The public political struggle that underwrote the Indian Mutiny was the colonial missionary urge to convert the heathen brown natives to Christianity, an encroachment that triggered a retaliatory insurrection, which besides deposing the British and their infidel religion sought to restore the ageing Mughal 'emperor' Bahadur Shah Zafar to the erstwhile seat of Mughal power in Delhi. *Junoon*'s opening scenes acknowledge those fiery Indian Muslim clerics who predicted the downfall of the accursed Christian British and inspired armed rebellion against them; such 'holy men' provided the divine sanctions necessary to legitimate the revolution's shocking violence. Importantly, their religious intervention served to combat the colonial myth of the white man's 'invincibility' by invoking a 'countermyth' of mystical divine powers which would aid the mutineers' aims.[1] These scenes serve a reminder the Great Indian Mutiny of 1857 – or the First Indian War of Independence – was a jihad triggered not by an inclusive nationalism but by parochial, religious, cultural and sectarian differences with the Christian outsider.[2] The private struggle within this public battle of colonial forces versus rebels is the obsession of a Muslim colonial subject for a Christian woman colonizer; he is defied by a white Christian woman whose identity significantly enables her resistance. Javed's 'love', an enduring, relentless obsession, thus founders on two rocks; he is not a white colonial, and he is not a Christian man. He is resisted by a woman who seeks to guard another woman's 'possessions', her young virginal body, to ensure it finds a 'rightful home' with a Christian white man. Javed 'wins' despite losing; for though Javed and Ruth do not find lives with each other, we learn Ruth died unwed, pining for her unrequited love.

In Ruskin Bond's novel, the heroine is not the young beautiful Ruth but rather, her widowed-by-the-Mutiny mother Mariam, who fiercely guards her daughter against the dangerous depredations of the natives. There, Ruth watches Mariam resist Javed's advances on herself and notes that 'Her eyes were bloodshot, staring out of their sockets . . . she presented a magnificent, and quite terrifying sight. . . . she frightened me even more than the man with the raised sword.'[3] Each male character responds to her demeanour and character with admiration and disbelief. Javed cannot withstand Mariam for 'he quailed under her stern gaze'[4] and says,[5]

> How can I describe the terror which seized me at the sight of her mother! Like an enraged tigress, whose side has been pierced by a barbed arrow, she hurled herself at me and presented her breast to my sword. I shall never forget the look she gave me as she thrust me away from the girl! I was awed. I was subdued. I was unmanned.

> The sword was ready to fall from my hand. Surely the blood of a hero runs through her veins! This is no ordinary female!

Mariam is clearly an exceptional woman of courage and self-possession, and yet, we wonder why an armed man is so nonplussed by a defiance that would easily succumb to the raised sword. *Junoon* answers: the crushing emasculations of colonialism have a great deal to answer for.

Junoon's opening scenes show the faded architectural glory of Awadh, home of a decadent royal dynasty of nawabs and 'a small cantonment town in the Indian plains'. We hear and see a devotional qawwali performed by a group of musicians and singers and see, in response, a mystic launch into a frenzied dervish's dance; Javed Khan, passing by on his horse, is halted in his tracks by this acute vision, this commingling of the lyrical, the passionate, the unhinged. The mystic's dance gestures at an irrationalism that underwrites the East, a spiritual and mystical kernel that resists the reason and the comprehension of the West. The mystic prophesizes a sea of blood of 'redcoat soldiers' at the end of the reign of a 100 years of the accursed *firanghees*, the British, who will suffer and take flight like pigeons to make their homes elsewhere;[6] this wild-eyed fakir thus anticipates and senses the violence of the Mutiny and the catastrophic chain of reprisal and retribution it set into motion. At the gathering potentially mutinous redcoat Indian soldiers are in attendance; among them is Sarfraz, a fiery organizer of a planned local revolt; in this venture Khan is reluctant to join.

Rumour of the impending revolt in the cantonment has spread into the homes of the British, of the Labadoors. At dinner, Mr Labadoor is sceptical the childlike sepoys are capable of rebellion; in the background, a sullen native continues to pull *pankah* as this assessment of his insurrectionary capacities does not deign to inquire into his opinions on its plausibility. At night, Ruth, who has become the subject of Javed Khan's obsession and infatuation, sees him outside her bedroom window, a lurking, mysterious figure signalling dangerous desire. The next day, at the Sunday services at the local church, the rebels attack and massacre the gathered English congregation, including Ruth's father. Ruth escapes and is rescued by Ramjimal, a loyal Indian friend who takes Ruth, Mariam and Ruth's grandmother home to his apprehensive family who fear reprisals from the rebels. Soon, Khan, searching for the target of his obsession, overcomes Ramjimal's defiance to seize the English women and moves them to his home, much to the displeasure of Firdaus, his beautiful wife. There, Khan makes the shocking announcement to his family he will protect women and children who suffer in war – by marrying Ruth. His witty aunt responds, 'Misfortune always falls on women in times of war; that is why war is honoured by men.' This dig at the masculine pretensions of the bold and blustering Pathan is a genuine masterpiece of script writing; its deployment by a brassy, bold woman unafraid to speak her mind renders it especially so. Here, in the intimate setting of a family gathering, a woman brings masculinity and its love for war to its knees.

Javed openly and ruefully confesses his unhinged, obsessive desire for Ruth, 'You don't understand the spell this girl has cast on me. I lost my senses when I saw her. I want this girl, and I will get her.' His obsession is impervious to insult or shaming; this love, like others before it, will not recognize moral, political or religious boundaries. The nature and form of Javed's infatuation with Ruth shows that sexual possession can seem incomplete for erotic, obsessive love; a more 'complete' dissolution of the self is sought in the public ritual of marriage, one possessing divine sanction and approval. Javed's singular obsession is best placed in counterpoint to his wife Firdaus's unrequited passion and sexuality, for her refusal to surrender her domestic and marital privileges, her compensations for marginalization in a patriarchal household, clash persistently with Javed's infatuation with Ruth. When Firdaus tries to seduce Javed at night, he is distracted and oblivious to her amorous advances; when she strokes him, he pushes her away, angering her. As Khan walks out into the darkness, Firdaus follows him; Khan walks along the passageway and looks across a corridor into the Labadoor's room as a plaintive song bemoans, 'Love has brought a catastrophe upon us, what will be its aftermath?' This masterful shot captures the obsessive and catastrophic nature of Javed's love for Ruth in showing characters displaying a complex web of allegiances and betrayals, each produced by, and productive of, the passions at play between Javed, Ruth, Mariam and Firdaus. But Javed acknowledges and bows down before Firdaus's gaze, for it is when he notices her presence that his staring at Ruth ends. As this scene powerfully demonstrates, Javed's obsessive lusting for Ruth can only be tempered by the presence of an even greater passion, Firdaus's fiery pride and jealous desire for her husband. Before this passion, even Javed's powerful obsession must take a step backwards.

Benegal, by showing the private's fissures – as evinced in Javed and Firdaus's conflicts, Javed's sharp tactical and strategic disagreements with Sarfraz, his running battles with Mariam – demonstrates that the public face of 1857s Mutiny, which speaks of a popular movement against English rule and of a fierce circling of the wagons by the British, was riven by its internal divisions and incoherences, by contested loyalties. Most prominently, Ruth's national, familial and religious obligations are placed under considerable stress by Javed's unrelenting, untiring passion. Ironically, Mariam's resistance to Javed's advances on her daughter allows him to repeatedly, publicly, proclaim his passion, to assert it is not merely a passing whim, to offer a vision of an enduring love to Ruth. Mariam will win the battle for her daughter's body but lose the war for her heart; she has engendered resistance to herself in her daughter and made impossible the further disposal of Ruth's life. For the patriarchal realities of the colonial world are such that for Ruth there is little difference between Javed, a brown Muslim man, and a white Christian suitor, perhaps a British Army officer, who will reduce her life to a dull clone of her mother's. A cloistered life awaits Ruth; she too will only be mistress of a household, reduced to managing its domestic particulars. Instead, Ruth gains access to a brown man – and the mysteries he represents – in the most mediated and moderated of ways; she receives repeated testimony of his undying passion for her, an otherwise dangerous force, which like an active volcano can only be observed safely at a distance. At night, Ruth dreams of Javed assaulting her, but we wonder whose desire is on display; for Ruth, too, Javed is a haunting vision of obsession, a creature of her dreams; we learn, if we did not already realize, that the colonial, exoticizing fascination goes in both directions.

The acute contrast between the public and the private of the Indian Mutiny is visible too, in Javed's stance towards the Indian rebellion. The attention Benegal pays to Khan's character emphasizes the complexity of the Mutiny's politics, which included actors and agents as diverse in their commitments to it as Javed and Sarfraz. Javed's primary allegiance in time of war is to a Christian, white woman; he is more interested in quietly and self-indulgently tending his pigeons while battle for his 'nation' rages elsewhere. (The symbolism of the captive pigeons for the Labadoors is obvious but not lacking in acuteness.) Javed's nominal interest in the Mutiny is only provoked when it becomes clear the fate of his love depends on its resolution. If waging battle and raising his sword will bring him the prize he seeks on the battlefield, his love, then India and its 'defenders' will find a true warrior, a true ghazi here. Otherwise, Javed is content with his petty existence, his tending of minor domestic affairs; the public and its contestations of nationalism and religion hold no attractions for him.

In sharp contrast, the fiery rebel Sarfraz's rhetoric invokes the rebel sepoy Mangal Pandey's failed rebellion against the use of cartridges smeared with pig and cow fat, the ruthless reprisals against mutinying soldiers by the cruel British, and angrily calls for self-assertion and violent retribution directed at the British. Sarfraz's rage is most visible in a dramatic segment when he, cursing and ranting, savagely destroys Khan's pigeon coops after returning defeated in the battle for Delhi; the pigeons are symbolic not just of the British but also of Javed's passiveness, his diverted passion; many were the Javeds in 1857 whose acquiescence and bystander status doomed the Mutiny.

Javed's greatest battles are with Mariam, the domestic representative of empire, as Javed and Mariam's contestation and negotiation for Ruth's body shows. Mariam invokes various constraints, real and imagined, to impose delays on Javed's insistence that Ruth and he marry: her mother's illness, the need for her brother's advice, the difficulty of inter-religious marriage. Javed and Mariam's dispute reaches a climax as he notes he could exert force to seize Ruth but is brought up short by Mariam:[7]

> Mariam: What if the British come back to power?
> Javed: They will hang me.
> Mariam: Do you want Ruth to become a widow?
> Javed: As if the British can come back. Delhi is with us.
> Mariam: Then let Delhi decide. If Delhi is yours, Ruth is yours.

Mariam has staked her fortunes on empire winning; the implacable material forces of empire are her strongest ally and she knows it; whatever might be her private resistance to *that* colonial, white, Christian patriarchy, she will not succumb to *this* brown, Indian, heathen one. Javed, aware of the awesome and awful power of the colonizer, one visible in its savage retaliations against mutineers, wishes to uncouple his desire from its power. When he suggests to Mariam the war between British forces and the rebels should not affect their 'personal relationships', Mariam accurately points out their current crisis has been created by the influence of the larger world upon their smaller one; its affairs cannot be conducted independent of it.

Junoon's conclusions display the final insult tendered by the public to the private. As colonial power asserts its dominance and quells the rebellion, the Labadoors and Khan's family, formerly residents of the same home, part ways to find refuge on their own. Javed, after returning from battle against the advancing British, desperately, obsessively, searches for Ruth and goes to the church where the Labadoor family are hiding. There, where it all began, he demands to be let in to see Ruth; he, retaining his sense of propriety, does not force his way in. Mariam tells Javed he has lost his wager and that his life is in danger from the approaching, vengeful British; he must leave. As Khan walks away crestfallen, defeated and resigned, Ruth runs out, and says but one word, 'Javed!' Their eyes lock, speaking volumes, and then Javed walks away, leaving Ruth alone, a tiny human figure set against the imposing impersonal figure of the church. Ruth and Javed alike are dwarfed by circumstance: love resists but cannot overcome the larger political forces of the world. A voice over epilogue informs us Javed died in battle while Ruth died fifty-five years later in London, unwed. We are left to grieve for Javed and Ruth's love, rescued by the boundaries that Javed's reticence drew around it, and destroyed by the colonial forces which laid waste to much else around the two lovers.

Junoon revels in the ambiguity of the colonial situation, the ambivalent love and hate, respect and contempt, the British and Indians felt for each other in the colonial era. The Labadoors' flight from refuge to refuge evokes the claustrophobia of British colonial existence in India: their persistent shielding from, their refusal to mingle with, to partake of, the world around them. For Ramjimal, their loyal friend, his personal ties to the English family outweigh any nationalist or religious inclinations; for his family, who are both apprehensive and xenophobic, and later, Javed's family, the British's political sins of colonialism appear less important than their violations of religious, moral and social orthodoxy. As a family friend points out in a pointed condemnation of the British, they wipe themselves with paper, their women dance with other men and do not cover their heads, and their soldiers committed a massacre of innocents in Kanpur. But personal relationships that transcend nationality, class and religion are only possible without the burdens of negotiating colonialism, which draws its own visible lines that limit the friendship between colonial subjects and colonizers: as Mariam and Ramjimal discuss plans for escape, Ramjimal touches Mariam's hand to offer reassurance, and she draws back as if stung; Ramjimal retreats, abashed at his violation of a previously sacrosanct boundary. He has been reminded, if ever so gently but firmly, that the British and Indians might share meals, owe each other money, save each other's lives, but an Indian man and a British woman cannot cross some carefully circumscribed boundaries. We learn, too, that a woman who cannot stand to have an Indian man touch her will under no circumstances permit her daughter to live her life with an Indian man.

Mariam and Javed's relationship symbolizes quite dramatically, the colonial British–Indian relationship, for they remain implacably opposed and unwilling to transgress self-imposed bounds of propriety in their interactions. *Junoon* revels in the inverted relationship between the colonizer and the colonized, who returns the former's exoticizing gaze, making the colonizer realize she is the object of the subaltern's curious attention, a physically weaker being possessing awesome material power. While Mariam sees the entire mysterious East gazing at her virginal, white, Christian daughter, Javed Pathan sees Mariam *and* her colonial power, a clue to understanding his perplexing interactions with her and Ruth. Why does Javed not simply assert his male dominance when seeking Ruth's hand in marriage? Javed's most forceful words to Mariam are merely, 'You are in mourning; you need time so take all you need, but don't dare show me your British impudence again.' Had Javed killed Mariam and raped Ruth, he would not have crossed the bounds of acceptable behaviour in that time and place; Ruth would have acquiesced eventually and become a 'good wife', an exotic 'keep', a 'bounty of war'. Instead Mariam remains defiant as Javed says, 'I want to marry your daughter legally. I will make her my wife in the right way; my religion permits it.' His path to Ruth hews to a carefully circumscribed trajectory of manners; he does not step out of its bounds, as he well might.

Javed's reticence in asserting his patriarchal authority is well understood by intersectional feminism: men do not always 'dominate' women of a politically and economically superior class; in particular, colonized men did not physically or materially dominate the women of their colonizers. In colonial India, very few Indian men 'took' white women; they were not allowed within touching distance of them. Indian men worked for white women with little opportunity to physically interact with their masters; they were not allowed access to their parlours and bedrooms. Some white women might have wished for a brown man to 'take' them, one so awed by their 'whiteness' that balance was restored in an otherwise skewed sexual power relation subject to patriarchal constraints; a 'capture' of one kind was a release of another. Javed can overpower Ruth with his physicality alone but he does not; he is held back, and this holding back is not merely the effect of Mariam's steely resolve or his aunt's taunting his Pathan manhood. Something else holds him back, perhaps the memory of how fiercely the white man guarded his precious womanly possessions; perhaps there lurks, in Javed's mind, a fear of the reprisals that would ensue were the Mutiny to fail. A dark truth of the Mutiny's violence was that Indian mutineers raped and killed English women; the savagery of the British response directed at the mutineers (and many other Indians) was commensurate with the terrible psychic injury colonial minds sustained in the rape and despoiling of 'white women'. All could be forgiven, but not the invasion of a white, Christian woman's body by the native. Javed seeking to win Ruth's hand by consensual marriage, a 'union' with Ruth in a form approved by her mother, rather than involuntary abduction and rape, is not just an expression of a chaste and proud love but also an insurance policy against a vengeful reprisal.

In Bond's novel, Javed is bound by a word of honour given to a Muslim holy man, a pir, that he will not harm the British women. The pir warns him to take care of his soul because he has taken an oath as a Pathan; he cannot expect to survive its betrayal.[8] In *Junoon*, this oath is no longer visible; Benegal leaves out this motivation for Javed's reticence to fully assert his masculine power, allowing for an interpretation in which a physically superior colonial man remains subjugated by the physically inferior white woman, unable and unwilling to assert his patriarchal privileges across colonial divides. This is the pathetic chivalry of the subaltern, too cowed by the colonial gaze to assert patriarchal and masculine superiority. Mariam's fierceness in defending Ruth is enabled by Javed; we see a man retreat when faced by a woman 'superior' to him in skin colour and her placement in the colonial world.

As in *Mammo*, women, whether British or Indian, find solidarity with each other in the sphere of private domesticity, cutting across lines of nationality and religion. When Firdaus makes clear her resentment and anger at the presence of the interloping Labadoor family in her home, Mariam speaks in Urdu, asking for acceptance and forgiveness, and acknowledging her patience and generosity in allowing them accommodation; the begum is pleasantly surprised, and indeed touched by Mariam's linguistic ability – a mark of acceptance of, and assimilation with, her own culture – and her hostility is partially assuaged. Mariam, an Anglo-Indian, resembles colonial India, a product of the intermarriage of England and India; she is fluent in two languages and can converse with both Javed and his begum in appropriate registers; she is thus able to form an informal alliance with Firdaus in disapproving of Javed's obsession. When Ruth washes her clothes by herself, she is helped by the women of the house; household work is the unifier between women of different race, caste, class and religion. As is their dependence on men, a sympathetic note is struck about the widowed Mariam by the Khan women in noting 'the woman who does not have a man is nothing'.

One beautiful, lyrical segment, in particular, captures the English and Indian women's friendship and mutual pleasure in their companionship. Javed's aunt arranges to take the Englishwomen to her home; they leave in palanquins as Ruth dances in the rain; like an Indian child, brought up in India, she is captivated by the wonders of the monsoon. As the women sing in a tree grove, and Ruth pushes Javed's cousin on a swing, we see a quiet scene of community between women, an oasis of personal peace from political strife. The English women sing an English song in good harmony while the Indian women watch with genuine pleasure; music here provides private moments of solidarity between English and Indian women, who both, in their respective cultures, are condemned to a life in the cloister of varying configurations. These scenes are especially powerful for their intense particularity: the women sing a song sung during the second month of the monsoon, shravan, while Mariam sings a song from Shakespeare.[9]

The deepest fear of the colonizer, as visible in Mariam's responses to Javed's advances on Ruth, was that intimate, personal familiarity with the colonized subaltern would offer damaging testimony to his humanity. Mariam knows this and attempts to weaken Javed's growing hold on Ruth's imagination. When her mother, Ruth's grandmother, says Javed is 'not a bad person', Mariam responds, 'You can never trust the enemy.' When a beaming Ruth, dressed in Indian clothes by her new Indian friends in Javed's home, asks her mother how she looks, Mariam snaps back, 'Like a nautch girl!' When a beaten Sarfraz returns from battle and encounters Mariam who accuses the mutineers of atrocities, and says, 'We've seen your humanity in the church' he snaps back, 'Yes, we worry only about the British because they have humanity, a name, an address, and an identity. But we don't. That is why they cut us like vegetables, burn our villages, kill our babies, all in the name of humanity.' Mariam's passionate resistance to the idea of humanity in the colonizer is of acute personal importance: Were familiar selves to be discovered there, then who knows which other defences, crucial for the maintenance of colonial, white, male, Christian supremacy, could come crumbling down? Would Mariam discover that she, too, was colonized, and had more in common with Javed than she might have imagined?

Suraj Ka Satwan Ghoda

Philosophy has long been concerned with fiction under two guises: the philosophy *of* literature and philosophy *in* literature. In *Suraj Ka Satwan Ghoda* (*The Seventh Horse of the Sun*, 1992), Benegal articulates both these concerns by offering an acute morally and politically inflected commentary on storytelling, storytellers, stories, fiction, fictional characters and fictional truth; it raises questions, and posits answers, about the relationship of literature and its characters to material circumstance. *The Seventh Horse* questions 'the very foundation of narrative experience . . . oral storytelling' through a series of stories 'told from shifting perspectives' by a neighbourhood's resident storyteller, Manek Mulla, and by employing through his listeners' commentary, an acute critical self-reflexivity.[10] *The Seventh Horse* thus employs a Rashômon-like narrative structure; its 'story' is understood as told three times by the same character who transforms himself into three different forms. Each story captures a 'facet' of the elusive 'diamond' – the supposed determinate meaning of the 'actual tale' being told; we may, of course, find there is no 'jewel in the crown' save the perspectives of the storyteller. E. M. Forster suggested in *A Passage to India* that the question of 'what really happened in the Marabar Caves' is far less interesting than an examination of how the perspectives of its characters are constructed and acquire internal coherence; there, too, we faced the wisdom of the injunction that there is no 'given' but only interpretation. Manek's stories are perspectives; our conventional failing is to seek for, to want to evaluate and assess, 'the actual story' that they are perspectives of; far more interesting, Benegal suggests, are the varying worlds generated by the divergent perspectives of those inhabiting 'the same story'.

As the story's listeners interrogate the storyteller, Manek, and the story and offer unsparing critique, we are exposed to the pleasures of the interactive text; Manek, the seemingly uncaring storyteller, is forced to have a moral conscience by his listeners and cannot maintain his detached-from-the-tale pose consistently; indeed, he is forced to change the form and content of his stories. The interrogation of the storyteller, the refusal of the listeners to accept the story as told, shows a story, its form and content alike, is negotiated by the storyteller and his audience. The storyteller, in sensing his audience's reaction, changes the story he wants to tell; the listeners become aware of their role in constructing the story they are about to hear and pass on. The story emerges at the nexus of the teller and listener; storytelling is not the mere 'faithful' transmission of extant text. And more is brought into being than just the tale, so too are the characters, their lives, their sensibilities, here now to challenge our notions of the 'real' and the 'fictional'.

Benegal's further attitude to stories and storytelling is captured in his claim it is impossible that 'the stories be separated from the storyteller' because 'you will always weave yourself into your stories'.[11] Manek Mulla's stories are ostensibly about 'others', women, with whom Manek was in love or who loved him; but Manek is always present, a persistent plot device in human form. *Suraj Ka Satwan Ghoda* thus enables a feminist reading: the story of women is told by men who weave themselves in self-serving ways into their narratives. The fate of women in *The Seventh Horse* is to have their stories told by a man who often seeks exculpation by revealing just enough to earn forgiveness from the listeners while casting himself as desirable enough to be the target of their love. In doing so, Manek reveals a great deal about himself, and indeed, about all men who inhabit women's lives, for the various characters he inhabits instantiate distinct and recognizable male archetypes.

Nietzsche asserted that philosophy is but disguised autobiography (a variant of which claim can be found in Benegal's claim above about the relationship between stories and storytellers). The converse is also true: autobiographies are expressions of values, morals, imperatives, claims about the nature of existence; they are, in short, philosophies. To know a person's philosophy, we must ask for his autobiography; what they choose to incorporate, to leave out, is theoretically significant. Different stories produce different selves; such is the therapeutic and self-constructing power of the narrative; the reason literary theory finds a welcoming home in psychoanalysis and psychotherapy. Manek Mulla's stories can be understood as autobiographies and thus therapeutic manoeuvres; his stories and storytelling are invested with personal political and moral significance for his project of constructing a dynamic personality for himself.

But the timelines of the stories recounted by Manek are not coherent and cannot be reconciled with each other if they are to be understood as narrative dimensions of the same person; instead, we are left to grapple with the possibility that the storyteller has merely borrowed characters and plots from differing tales, treating them as reusable entities in the service of the storytelling craft and in an ambiguous project of self-construction. Manek Mulla's stories can, indeed, be understood as separate tales with little compulsion to reconcile their timelines and plots. As we find ourselves doing, driven to make narratives cohere according to our compulsions and felt needs. Much as those recounting the stories of their lives do; Manek's disdain for such consistency renders his self-indeterminate and places in question the success of his narrative and existential enterprise. Or perhaps there are more varieties of self-construction and selves enabled by storytelling than we conventionally allow.

The Seventh Horse's fundamental structure is reflexive: we commence watching a movie; we see a man reminisce and go on to tell a story, in flashback, about a storyteller who tells four stories in flashback, each questioned by a group of listeners, which includes our original storyteller. The dialogue between the storyteller and his listeners contains political and literary rumination; we sense the articulation of a distinct philosophical position on the relationship between film and fiction and truth and love, a relationship attenuated, altered and modified by the material environment of politics and social structure. The storytelling often takes place inside Manek's room, in a small, intimate setting, typical of the neighbourhood 'hangout' or adda, the venue for 'barbershop' conversation; this allows Benegal to generate an acute visual contrast between the privacy and enclosure of the storytelling venue and the expansive reach of the story and its perennial themes 'outside'. (In one curious scene, after Manek's listeners leave for the night, thunder and lightning light up the sky as Manek closes up for the night. There is a hint here of the natural order of the world disturbed by the 'falsehoods' of the story told by the storyteller. Are the gods angered by the arrogance and insolence of man become creator and dispenser of fates?)

In the first couplet of stories, Manek is a schoolboy wearing shorts, a passive observer of his beautiful neighbour Jamuna's romance with Tanna, a meek man dominated by his overbearing father. Jamuna's parents consider Tanna's family's caste and income beneath theirs; Jamuna is married off to an older, infirm landlord who does not need dowry and can promise his estate as an inheritance to his young bride and their possible offspring. Unable to bear children because of her husband's advancing years, Jamuna has a child through his manservant, the charming story of which encounter contains a sharp political moral about unconventional acquisitions of power, about how the working classes can subvert their masters' homes, at its heart. Jamuna's tale speaks, too, to a perennial Indian problem of poverty and its resultant social evils of dowry and tragedies of unrequited love, deception and loveless marriages. Jamuna's story is not just one of failed romance; it shows how social and economic pathology can ruin love.

The material compulsions and constraints that drove Jamuna into the home of the landlord continue to drive her life onwards in Manek's second tale. We see a married Jamuna visiting her parents from her new home with her older, landlord husband; after recounting stories of how her husband's previous wives had 'looted' him, she claims, falsely, that she cannot help her desperate parents financially; thanks to her marriage and her new loyalties, her economic interests and personal concerns have diverged from those of her parents. Now, she is more concerned to maintain the feudal estate's financial integrity. She has grown apart from Tanna too; his fates find their own tragic resolution as he fails to find love or happiness in his marriage to another woman, Lily.

In another set of stories, Manek restricts himself to recounting the events contained within a twenty-four-hour span so that he will not have to supply 'excessive' plot and narrative detail; the storyteller can afford to be selective in this manner of recounting stories so that their coherence cannot be questioned. In its first instalment, we see Lily, a prosperous young woman, and Manek, now cast as an accomplished, prosperous and sophisticated writer, are romantically involved, but she is to be married to Tanna. (Some unnamed compulsion, perhaps familial, perhaps economic, ensures Lily will be married off, a fact she tearfully mourns.) Their conversation suggests Jamuna is the fictional creation of the writer Manek; Manek reads out parts of a story to Lily, suggesting she emulate its characters in her response to her current predicament. Should we indeed seek out literature and literary characters to derive moral lessons for our lives? To complete the dream-like quality of this tale, the two sing a song – a traditional Indian film industry trope – in the falling rain. Lily is then shown getting married to Tanna with Manek a melancholic attendee. We are bewildered: How has Manek changed his age, prosperity and intellectual maturity so while Tanna and Lily remain chronologically frozen? What is Jamuna's being? Is she merely a fantasy dreamed up by the writerly Manek? And what, of course, is the relationship between Manek the writer that we see in the story and the Manek who is the storyteller, possessed of considerably less comfortable economic and material circumstances in his modest one-room apartment?

In the last story we encounter Sati, a young soap-selling woman (who has been visible in the earlier stories). Now, Manek is a boy again, a budding poet, and the subject of a romantic interest directed at him by Sati. But Sati's love is doomed by Manek's indifference, apathy and cowardice. Shamefully, Manek stands by while Sati is assaulted by Tanna's lecherous father after being 'sold off' to him by her foster father; he can only listen stoically, all the while worried he will be asked to tender assistance to this 'damsel in distress'; Manek remains too ashamed of social disrepute to aid her. His primary concerns are to secure a degree and then a paying job; the bourgeois hankering for respectability leaves no time for moral action or political sympathy. When Sati seeks Manek's help to escape from home, imagining their 'connection' to be underwritten by a romantic attraction, he turns her back over to her rapist. Manek's physical and moral cowardice, induced by conformity to caste and class expectations, underwrite this betrayal. Our narrator informs us that that was the last day he saw Manek; he himself, inspired by Manek's storytelling, went on to become a writer of stories. Like the one he has just told us. We learn the effect of Manek's storytelling on him is to stimulate his vivid imagination and his desire to tell stories in turn; thus do stories 'produce' or 'generate' other stories in response.

The *Seventh Horse of the Sun* offers a sharp critique of conventional understandings of romantic love. Bharati's original novel undermines an Indian romantic archetype, the Indian Werther, Devdas, the lovelorn hero of popular Indian legend and cinema who drowns his sorrows in alcohol after being denied his true love, the courtesan Paro.[12] But Manek and his listeners express scorn for Devdas, a conventional love story which possesses only one 'ending': the 'heroine' marries someone else and the 'hero' is left bereft and heartbroken. Manek insists a good love story should 'uplift society'; his tales are not the conventional tragedies of unrequited love. Here, love fails, but Manek is not Devdas; in each case, the woman in question is his, but he chooses to spurn their love; here, too, we find love is not independent of the socio-economic conditions in which it is to take root and flourish.

In *The Seventh Horse*, love features in the contestation between the material and the romantic; the fleeting glimpses we catch of it in its triumphant moments are the ones that convince the poets of its primacy, the political theorist of its valence. But otherwise, its efficacy and primacy are contested; one listener rejects the pre-eminence of love in human affairs, and suggests it is grossly overestimated both in its placement and in its efficacy; actual lives leave little time for love. As he notes, 'Love is not eternal, and it competes for all time with all the other tasks a man must accomplish in his life. Indeed, there is little time left for real romantic love, which forms such a small part of our lives. Why then, do we devote so much attention to it?'

As Benegal and Bharti note, love is transformed and attenuated by the materiality of the world around it; Manek's romantic failures are not driven by personal, emotional responses to the women he knows but by his responses to the material world; his moral sense is debilitated by its constraints. Manek's social and economic advancement, his 'upward mobility', is only possible if he pursues his studies to obtain the desired 'credentials' for the 'job market'; the care and maintenance of romantic relationships is secondary to such considerations. Romance will come of its own accord when material advancement is secured.

The Seventh Horse asserts the derivative Marxist claim that the love story must fulfil some reformist function; otherwise, it is mere bourgeois distraction and beguilement. Can love, described as the strongest force of all, really overcome materiality and material circumstances? No, the Marxist storyteller insists, true love can only find a smooth path when class struggle has ceased. Manek's stories therefore heap scorn on the idea that romantic love can transcend class struggle; the love story appears a piece of classist ideology in insisting the world of desire remains as it was before a class structure was imposed on it, deluding us into thinking it is possible to find uncommodified love. The class-insensitive storyteller is a bourgeois stooge then, propping up a reactionary class order with misleading stories of unassailable and impervious love. Marriage, that summum bonum of romantic love, turns out to have a history, to possess cultural variations; it has served to preserve and promote particular economic states of affairs. Far from being a divinely exalted and sanctified expression of the love of man for woman (or vice versa), marriage is infected with the profane. Manek's stories of love, rather than being stories of spiritual redemption, are stories of disappointment, of thwarted desire, dashed on the rocks of unbending and unyielding material realities, unsympathetic to the desires of the heart. In *The Seventh Horse* love does not overcome the caste system, the constraints of the family system or the credential-seeking job market. (Elsewhere, cultures of work, of unbending commitment to the workplace, do not produce sensibilities conducive to romantic, sexual love; when they do, the love they produce is commodified. As parents find out, sexual love succumbs all too easily to the trials and travails of expensive, exhausting, time-consuming parenting. Those parents who can afford to pay for help find their romance flourishes; a paid nanny's labour saves the marriage, not romantic love's undying expressions or courtship; the parents' romantic date becomes possible because the babysitter's labour facilitates it. The bodies of others, their labour, must be pressed into service for our bodies to find expression in romantic, sexual love.)

However, *The Seventh Horse of the Sun* does suggest that though compared to the unbending material reality of the public 'outside', the private's indulgences in romance and flirtation appear frivolous and weak-willed, the private may still assert itself with a vengeance in the public sphere. As Manek's listeners point out, in Jamuna's story, a working man, an estate servant, makes his child the heir to a zamindar's fortune by securing entry to the master's most private chambers and 'possessions', by providing a glimpse of a 'true love' to a woman married against her will. In such fashion love may subvert the systemic class and economic constraints that enclose and constrain it.

The Seventh Horse (along with *Trikaal*) represents a concerted effort by Benegal to explore the puzzles of temporality as within the stories of Jamuna, Lily and Sati, Manek's character makes leaps along his world timeline even as other characters move sedately along theirs. Who is the real Manek Mulla and what was his age and romantic maturity? The adult Manek can be explained as the storyteller's stand-in for the man who was Lily's love before she was reluctantly married to Tanna; this seems a wholly imagined construction on Manek's part, a filling in of a blank into which he inserts himself, fashioning himself into a sophisticated writer possessing a beautiful woman whom he can leave aside for her wedding. But we are not sure what to make of the older boy who abandons Sati, and why he is portrayed as such a moral coward and a boor. For Manek's stories offer exculpations of past acts and indictments too. There is sophistication in Manek's character but considerable moral cowardice, too, which Manek does not bother to hide. Diverse motives could underlie such unflattering frankness on Manek's part. One crucial one is to portray critical moral trajectories of 'improvement'; if we have always been angels then the moral arc of our life is uninteresting. We tell stories for many reasons; Manek's are placed in the service of a distinctive craft of self-construction.

Though the storyteller in *The Seventh Horse* is a man, the central characters are women, for it is around their stories the crises of the movie emerge. These women express defiance even as they cannot ultimately resist patriarchy and male power: the frivolous Jamuna, inspired by fantasies of pulp romantic novels – there is a touch of Madame Bovary here – conducts love with whichever man offers her comfort and solace; Lily is proud enough to leave Tanna though we detect cruelty and impatience in her dealings with her husband; while Sati, a bold and brassy woman who flourishes a knife at her harassers, is finally done in by collaborative violence and indifference. The women's names reflect their background and fate: Jamuna's destiny is to be merged into a larger whole (the holy rivers Ganga and Jamuna merge as the Ganga heads to the ocean); Lily's anglicized name reflects her beauty and affluence; while the unfortunate Sati is the sacrifice made to patriarchy. Each woman is disposed of by her family: Jamuna is married off to an older man; Lily is married to a man she does not and cannot love; Sati is disposed of as chattel by her caretaker. The stories of Jamuna, Lily and Sati could have been told by removing Manek's multiple characters and making a 'conventional Benegal movie'. But Benegal's storytelling and his philosophical and cinematic choices allow him instead to reiterate the theses of a socially, politically and psychologically realist movie in an experimental wrapper. Though such is not the conventional understanding of *The Seventh Horse*, here, too, Benegal has unerringly found the opportunity to make a feminist statement.

Bharati's introduction to his novel makes clear its political subtext, its Marxist framing of class structures interacting to produce social and psychological realities. Critical reactions to *The Seventh Horse* stress its avant-garde leanings but often elide the material critique Bharati and Benegal level at Indian social institutions like the family, the caste system and dowry, and the resultant economic 'burden' that women 'impose' on their families, which plays a crucial role in the resolution of women's lives by chattel-like treatment. It is tempting to view *The Seventh Horse* as purely an opportunity for postmodernist reflection on the nature of cinema and literature and their created worlds. But that would be to ignore its political, social and ethical claims, the discomfort it produces in our reckoning of the fates of its characters.

Kondura

If Benegal's 'uprising trilogy' was occasionally optimistic despite its sombre descriptions of dysfunctional Indian hinterlands, *Kondura* (The Sage from the Sea, 1978), a tale set in those same precincts, is avowedly pessimistic. *Kondura* recounts the tale of a 'failed uprising', one that could call upon divine forces to achieve earthly change but which ran aground on a confused understanding of its distinctive powers and political capacities and its fatal susceptibility to the earthly pathology of patriarchy. *Kondura* bears strong structural and narrative affinities with Satyajit Ray's tragic masterpiece *Devi* (1960) in which a young woman is 'appointed' as the reincarnation of the Mother Goddess by her father-in-law; both movies move between reality and fantasy with ease as the divine and the sacred mingle with the secular and the profane. Both these 'encounters' of the earthly and the divine end in tragedy as the heavenly and the profane find coexistence intractable; in each case, a woman pays the price of this irreconcilability; in *Kondura*, we catch a tantalizing glimpse of how myth, 'magic' and superstition can be revolutionary, possibly bringing real, tangible deliverance to the faithful but are defeated instead by human cowardice and ignorance.

The mingling of the sacred and the secular in Ray's *Devi* and Benegal's *Kondura* was well understood by Indian audiences, who bring these together in their weekday worlds in prayers and daily invocations and rituals, and more importantly, in enduring beliefs that acknowledge the immanence of the divine and the supernatural.

In *Devi*, the members of a petit bourgeois family reconcile themselves to the supposed transformation of a mere woman into a reincarnation of a goddess; in *Kondura*, villagers are prepared to believe the divine can visit them in the form of a god-man or saint, that the magical is around and in them, manifest in the powers of the saint and his interactions with empirical realities, that the weak are transformed into the strong by the intervention of supernatural powers, that divine curses have earthly valence, that the affairs of man can be disposed of by God *and* his chosen human agents. In both cases, these beliefs, as rules for action, lead to choices and decisions with catastrophic consequences. One interpretive conclusion to draw is that the very beliefs which drove such choices were 'mistaken' or 'false'; the other is that the wrong choices were among the many actions those beliefs suggested as possibilities. Beliefs are rules for actions, but the actions they pick out are not unique, because those beliefs interact with other pre-existent ones; in *Kondura*, we see how a supposed saint's beliefs in his magical powers interacts, fatally, with his beliefs about women and their sexuality. Human agents act on the basis of choices; in both *Devi* and *Kondura*, the 'wrong' choices are made. In both cases, because men have forced their beliefs about women into predetermined containers of thought. *Devi* and *Kondura* are often interpreted as 'reformist cinema', striving to cure India of its 'primitive superstitions', its 'simplistic faith in the supernatural', but they are feminist tracts as well, for the attention they force us to pay to the fates of their women characters. Woman, too, is the object of superstitious, sometimes fatal, understandings of her capacities and abilities and desires; patriarchy is a superstition all its own.

Ray and Benegal make the ironic point that the granting of 'goddess status' to women as a notable Indian cultural construction is a curse; though seemingly indicating a profound, respectful estimation of female divinity as a distinctive cultural signature, a homage to the divine feminine archetypes that supposedly animate Indian thought and mythology, such grants ignore the uncomfortable truth that here, too, class and caste are relentless accompaniments to all Indian social formations, that 'poor and lower-caste women were far from being considered "goddesses"' and that there were many 'problematic implications of "goddess" status for women of middle-class families'.[13] Not the least of which was a politically convenient denial of their earthly powers and rights in favour of granting them wholly imagined divine ones. In both *Devi* and *Kondura*, the granting of divinity is not a blessing for 'goddesses' enmeshed in patriarchal understandings of their powers, capacities and virtues; the female divine, too, it is suggested, must give way to profane self-interested patriarchy, especially in cultures where feminine power is most comfortably accepted when it flows from distant, divine sources, and where male conceptions of feminine power are grounded in patriarchal stereotypes. Goddesses, too, turn out to be sexually pure, and chaste, and obedient to their male consorts. Benegal and Ray thus suggest the liberation of women will not be aided by divine forces but by the marshalling of earthly ones; more pessimistically, these movies claim that the political salvation of women lies beyond the reach of patriarchal men and societies. Even if, on occasion, they are considered divine.

Kondura centres its narrative on the notion of a 'religious experience', which is 'noetic' and 'authoritative'[14] and results in a 'new world' for its central protagonist Parshuram (Anant Nag). Like others before him in other times and places and eras, Parshuram has this religious experience at a time of acute emotional crisis – in his case, as he abandons his family and home, heading to the seashore, where journeys begin, and ships are wrecked; it is where the 'solid' land meets the 'restless' ocean. The turmoil of this encounter mirrors that in Parshuram's mind, for domestic discord has pushed him here, protesting an invasion of his intimate life by his extended family. He is determined to show himself worthy of respect by his family, to make his wife happy and fill his house with children, a desire that will be negated by the 'boon' soon to be granted him. Parshuram dreams of acquiring power, of 'going on a journey'; he spins out fantasies of redemption and vindication. As he strides on, he is called to by a wild-eyed sage, the mythical Kondura, who stands on a cliff:[15]

> Kondura: Where are you going?
> Parshuram: Where this path takes me.
> Kondura: Your path is decided. Go back. Much has to be done by you. Give this root to whom it is to be given. An abortion will take place. For this to work, you must remain celibate.

Parshuram accepts this 'boon' and turns back. A group of black pigs crosses his path; he considers this a bad omen but 'decides' he has seen both good and bad omens on the same day, and presses on. This is selective, interest-and-outcome oriented understanding and interpretation: the black pigs are, in a naturalistic light, merely animals crossing a path; in the light of an ancient superstition they are a bad omen, but that superstition itself can be countered by another imperative, which now settled on a new purpose, helps construct alternative, self-interested interpretations of empirical phenomena. This is a new consciousness, and a new being, set astride in a new world, with a new moral and political order.

But this religious experience is only partially effective in bringing about a transformation of Parshuram, who tests Kondura's power by searching for water outside his family home; water is indeed found, a dramatic confirmation. With Kondura's power corroborated, Parshuram receives and interprets signals and emanations from a charged environment; he has been 'converted' and lives among new emotional, moral and metaphysical realities. At night, he hears bells ringing at the local temple, but his wife cannot hear them; in the temple, he is offered incontrovertible evidence its bells do not move, but he continues to hear them ringing. The temple priest warns him not to sleep in the temple because 'The Goddess comes at night – if you see her, you will lose your eyes.' We understand this metaphorically: Parshuram will acquire a 'new vision'. As he already has, through his visions of the Goddess who 'speaks' to him; the bells are her bidding.

Parshuram soon sees his wife Anusuya appear as the Goddess in the temple; Parshuram has decked out his 'visions' in human form. When at night, the bells ring again and beckon Parshuram to the temple, his wife sees him leave; we see her shadow on the wall as he does. In this cave-like allegory, under the spell of Kondura's boon, Parshuram only sees a shadow of his wife. Benegal suggests that Parshuram does not see 'better' but 'worse' under Kondura's spell; here is not revelation, but delusion, one sustained by Parshuram's prior beliefs about Anusuya, who is understood as either the fatal temptress of sexual attraction, undermining his vows of celibacy, or a denatured, asexual Goddess; there is no place here for an understanding of Anusuya as a 'mere woman'. Parshuram shares his belief that the Goddess's spirit inhabits her with Anusuya herself, who, stranded on the other side of this 'divide', cannot comprehend the ontological and epistemological contours of the world Parshuram now inhabits; he acquires his beliefs and their justifications from sources wholly unknown to her.

During her visitations, the Devi (Goddess) says to Parshuram, 'Sin is increasing everywhere; there will be misfortune. You must reconstruct the village temple' but remains silent in response to his question, 'Where will I get money from?' The next morning, on seeing the landlord's cart, his answer is at hand; the world is full of meaningful signs for the believer, the convert. Parshuram convinces the village's rapacious and lustful landlord Bhairav Murthy – a variant of Anna in *Nishant* – that he must pay for the reconstruction; the temple priest, as the earthly representative of heavenly powers but subservient to the landlord, must acknowledge the material power of earthly realities and fall in line too. The villagers for their part are convinced that a new prophet is at hand; they come seeking spiritual deliverance and guidance from Parshuram; his star is ascendant and he becomes a new 'saint' in the village, one who challenges and 'displaces' the priest and the landlord, the former loci of control in this land.

The Devi's insistent and dire warnings that 'sin' in the village is ascendant convince Parshuram that the 'sinner' is the zamindar, responsible for the 'growing sin' in his crippled nephew Vasu's beautiful wife Parvati for she is now pregnant. Convinced the child to be born to Parvati is the landlord's – the product of 'sin' – and not Vasu's, Parshuram insists on feeding prasad (divine offerings to the gods) made from the root to Parvati. The 'poison' of the root dispensed, the zamindar informs the horrified Parshuram the baby was indeed Vasu's. Dogs howl as Parshuram runs to the temple to beg for forgiveness; at home, Parshuram confesses his sins to Anusuya, the imagined human form of the Goddess, and falls at her feet, saying, 'If I have sinned, then if I sin again, it will wipe that out', a convoluted logic of absolution which serves to justify his subsequent rape of Anusuya. During the rape, we see Anusuya's anguished expression; Benegal moves his lens away to capture the woman's experience of her violation, not the titillation provided by the act of violent, forced sexual intercourse. Parshuram awakens to find the bells have stopped ringing – symbolizing the end of the Devi's 'spell' – and Anusuya dead at the bottom of a well, her life ended at her own hands, a cruel resolution of the sense of confusion, betrayal and trauma that has been visited upon a woman victimized by her husband. Parshuram returns to the shore, where it all began, screaming, 'Kondura, what has happened?' The answer is evident to all but Parshuram, who like Oedipus, thought he knew too much and turned out to know very little.

In *Kondura*, Benegal suggests that 'the real' is that which animates agency and has political and moral valence. It is pointless to ask whether Parshuram is 'merely delusional' or 'actually experiencing' his visions of the Devi; what matters is whether a human agent can be galvanized into action by such experiences. Benegal suggests legends and myths and 'mere stories' which mingle the spiritual and the material survive and flourish because they are *effective*; they have a pragmatic value; they act as enablers of political action, of the taking of moral stances. The unimaginative atheist reckons religion consists of fantasies or hallucinations, but the test of the 'reality' of religious and spiritual belief lies elsewhere: What actions does this belief commit us to? What rules of actions do such beliefs supply? Such pragmatist concern for the 'effective' value of a philosophical concept, the efficacy of a 'vocabulary' in directing action in *Kondura*, suggests 'existence' and 'reality' are contested notions, for indeed, the existence of Kondura, the Goddess, the efficacy of the boon granted Parshuram, the reality of his visions, are not to be determined by simple acts of verification. Instead, metaphysics and epistemology merge here; no statement of knowledge is made without indexing the epistemic subject making the claim – in this case, Parshuram.

What exists for Parshuram is a function of his best theory of the world and his 'priming'; such claims are not independent of his history of upbringing in a devout, Brahmin household, and the environment in which he functions and finds a receptive audience – the villagers and his family – that confirms and establishes his power. Parshuram and the villagers devoted to him reside within interconnected networks of meaning in which the provision of certain kinds of reasons can galvanize the moral and political subject; the efficacy of their beliefs is a function of their location in these networks. Are the beliefs in the reality of Kondura, the Goddess, her powers and the power of Kondura justified? The answer lies in what those beliefs 'do' for those who hold them; the villagers seek answers to life's perplexities, of whatever nature, and Kondura's agent has 'answers'. Benegal suggests then that communication with, and the persuasion of, those who possess different world orders does not proceed by attacking the foundations of their beliefs or their ontological or epistemic claims; rather we paint an alternative picture of a 'better' world – in the moral, political or aesthetic dimensions – obtainable by the practical, action-inducing adoption of the alternative conceptual scheme. Parshuram has within him the power to generate such an image, and to realize it through the adoption by the villagers of the belief that he is Kondura's agent, one worthy of pledging allegiance to; the tragedy of *Kondura* is that his power is so fatally misdirected.

It would be a reductive mistake to consider *Kondura* a simple condemnation of village superstition and a call to modernity to invade the 'backwards' precincts its characters inhabit. A militant atheist might shake his head at the 'ignorance' and 'illiteracy' on display by Parshuram, the villagers, his family, but a more perspicuous spectator would note the potential for radical political change contained in the 'superstitious' beliefs Parshuram professes – the power of the landlord and the priest are both threatened by that of the new prophet because their 'former followers', the villagers, have found a new leader. If *Kondura*'s end is ultimately tragic, it is because the desired outcomes have not obtained by the deployment of these supposedly 'superstitious beliefs'; the landlord's power – the real 'sin' that is growing unchecked in the village – remains untouched, Parvati's child is aborted, Anusuya kills herself and Parshuram is left bereft. And the village's central pathologies, those of feudal rule, remain unchecked.

We can imagine a *Kondura* in which the new 'saint' commands the villagers to revolt against the evil landlord and overthrow his power for *Kondura* depicts a 'prophet' who could have realized a political vision directed by sacral intervention. In this 'liberatory theology', Moses, Christ and Mohammed were Parshuram's precursors: revolutionary prophets who upset established social and political orders through the artful deployment of sacral visions and revelations; the most disappointing prophets are not those who traffic in 'myths' but those who prop up established regimes of power, who realize no earthly change despite having heavenly sanction. Kondura and the Devi granted Parshuram real, tangible power in the here and now, visible in his interactions with the three loci of power in the village: the landlord, the priest and the villagers themselves – *Kondura* is the story of Parshuram's failure to realize that power. When Parshuram informs the zamindar of the Devi's omen and insists the reconstruction of the temple is his responsibility, the zamindar promptly calls for his aide to start work. Later we witness the supplication of the women of the landlord's house who ask Parshuram for his blessings and seek to feed him, and Parshuram riding the landlord's car home after his first audience at the feudal estate – an act visible to all the villagers. These are dramatic indicators of Parshuram's new power and its capacity to alter material realities.

The new prophet has, unwittingly, a populist bent and, convinced he is Kondura's 'agent', is not hesitant to use his newly acquired confidence and self-possession. When local construction workers ask for half of the temple's proceeds as payment for their labour on the new premises, Parshuram agrees and overrides the temple priest's long-established authority to decide such matters. When villagers come to obtain the new swami's darshan and are ordered by the priest to perform their prayers on the idol in the temple's yard instead, Parshuram grants them an audience, overriding the priest's authority.

When the priest objects that the zamindar's permission is needed for these prayers, the villagers defer to Parshuram instead – a sign that power has been transferred to a newer loci. This new power is iconoclastic too, for the older idol outside the temple is destroyed in the course of the temple's construction – a permission granted by the landlord to Parshuram.

Parshuram's power is visible most dramatically, in the devotion tendered him by the villagers as prayer meetings and fairs spring up. Parshuram's new power alters his personal relationships too: his family, his formerly sceptical brother included, acknowledge his authority and holiness. At home, his wife washes his feet and his family offers him the same obeisance they might offer to distant gods, seeking forgiveness for their earlier failure to recognize his sainthood. His family bathes in the water with which he has washed his feet: humility, devotion and self-effacement are present in this ritual of the merger with the body of the saint.

But Parshuram's power is ultimately, disastrously, employed with murderous inaccuracy: Parvati's pregnancy is aborted, Anusuya is raped and the zamindar is left free to abduct and assault the village women as before. Parshuram's fatal mistake is to not realize the rapacious power of the landlord is the true evil that stalks the land; this failure is aided by a misunderstanding and underestimation of a woman's sexuality, of Parvati's ability to find a relationship with her crippled husband Vasu that is not limited by Parshuram's conceptions it. On his first visit to the landlord's home, Parshuram was shocked and repelled to see the beautiful Parvati married to the disabled Vasu; his distaste for Vasu remains an obsession which ensures he fails to notice the landlord's active pathologies, for Murthy is a rapacious exploiter of the women of the village, who consider rape by the landlord an unavoidable aspect of their life. The inability to make a political ally of a woman is the true strategic and tactical moral and political failure here, a failure stemming from Parshuram's fatal lack of knowledge about women.

Towards Parvati, Parshuram's attitudes are wholly patriarchal; he cannot accept her consensual sex with Vasu because of his lack of sexual imagination, and he stands ready to condemn a pregnancy that might have resulted from her rape by Murthy. At no point does Parshuram consider asking Parvati how she might choose to 'dispose' of her pregnancy; her desires are irrelevant. The zamindar casts aspersions on Parvati's pregnancy, too, calling her a 'casteless whore' mothering an illegitimate child; her resistance to his power, manifest in a spirited defence of Vasu whom he had violently assaulted, makes her worthy of this abuse. Both Parshuram and the landlord question the woman's pregnancy, unwilling and unable to imagine that her sexuality – and that of her husband's – is not circumscribed by their impoverished male imagination. In their patriarchal attitudes, Parshuram and Murthy are united.

Parshuram's sexual obsession with Parvati, Anusuya's bewildered reactions to his self-imposed celibacy and his sexual denial are the price he must pay for his 'boon', a torment not eased with the possession of problematic temporal power. While Parshuram claims to embrace the powers of the root, it is evident Parshuram hopes he will be released from this ambiguous 'boon'. For Parshuram shrinks from the possibility that the root is efficacious: if it is not, he will be released from the burden of his celibacy and from the responsibility of having to exercise its concomitant power. At home, when the beautiful and sensuous Anusuya had invited Parshuram into their bedroom, his invocation of the constraints of his 'vow' prompted him to confess he considered the boon a curse – it does deny him his sexuality:[16]

> Anusuya: Don't you like me? Why are you punishing me? What will people think? It is better that I die.

Parshuram: You are not being punished. This is my test.

Anusuya: Test? Who is giving this test to you?

Parshuram: Kondura. He has cursed me and bound me. It will be good if the water does not appear; it will prove the root does not have power.

Power, here described as a 'curse' and not a 'boon', is not always welcome; with it comes judgement, choice, culpability. Better to remain powerless, to be moved around like a pawn, rather than face askance for choices and decisions. Benegal thus establishes a deeper political point: revolutions fail because revolutionaries shrink from power, appalled by the responsibility to be thrust upon them, by the loss of freedom implicated in the exercise of political power. Rebels know the king is a lonely person, and much as they resent his power, they are not envious of his isolation, his subjection to judgement; this is a throne they shrink from occupying.

Kondura comes to Parshuram at a time of 'crisis': Parshuram has left home because of the unbearable pressures of his domestic strife; it is at that moment the 'sage speaks'; the boon granted, and the condition imposed, are unsurprising within the indicated cultural context. Sexual celibacy as a 'conserver' and indeed, 'enhancer and amplifier' of spiritual and personal power finds extensive textual support in Hindu scriptures and mythology, indicating acute religious and moral commitment result from self-denial and abnegation; a Brahmin like Parshuram who sets himself on a new course of determined action plausibly invokes this rigorous modality of 'self-discipline'. The great ascetic sages and warriors of Indian myths meditated in order to gain boons from the gods; their efforts were marked, most distinctively, by their commitments to celibacy. When the gods sought to disturb them, recognizing a force that could destabilize the heavens and threaten their divine power, they disrupted their meditative trances by sending beautiful damsels, apsaras, as distractions of sexual desire. Even the demon king Ravana attained his demonic powers through his commitments to celibacy; his failure to resist his sexual desire for Sita, consort of the divine king, Rama, was the key to his vanquishment by Rama.

The Hindu notion of 'sankalp' – 'an intention formed by the heart and mind, a singular resolve directed at a specific goal, a tool to harness the will, to focus and harmonize mind and body' – is relevant in understanding Parshuram's behaviour; for he understands his vision of Kondura as demanding celibacy as a symbol of his commitment, his sankalp. Parshuram has realized his earthly limitations and seeks to transcend them; he distrusts his corporeal body and its desires and passions which weaken him; strength will come when he will resist the most visceral temptation of all as a proof of his determination. Celibacy is the strongest and most visible expression of his sankalp; to embrace it is to find a path beyond the trap of his current existence. Parshuram does not realize his 'boon' cannot rescue him from himself; the same faults which led to his family finding disfavour with him are the ones that engender the catastrophic misunderstanding that lead him to cause Parvati to have a miscarriage, to deny his wife the happiness of their marital chambers and the possibility of a child, to rape her and drive her to death.

The timing and placement of Parshuram's vision of Kondura is not accidental. If he is indeed running away from home, why is he not on a road heading elsewhere? Instead, he heads directly to the ocean, the established residence of the sage by the sea. Psychoanalytically, Parshuram's actions betray his inner world; Parshuram does not intend to commit suicide; he is engaged in an act of resolve instead. He is psychologically primed to 'find', to 'see', a divine, supernatural vindication of his sankalp. He needs a belief to convince him of his passage to self-determination; he finds a supernatural, other-worldly foundation, one created by his own needs, the sage who stands on the cliff and gives him a 'magical root'. It is crucial to not use the language of delusion or hallucination in describing Parshuram's experiences; Parshuram does 'see' Kondura as indeed, he does 'see' the Devi in the temple; for him, as for us, 'believing is seeing'. It is no coincidence the Devi comes in the form of his wife; the viewer of the vision must translate the form of the Goddess, the divine energy, into a form understandable to him; correspondingly, the divine energy must render itself into a form comprehensible to its recipient. Parshuram's desires drape and deck out Kondura in human form; they translate, too, Anusuya into the form of the Goddess. Parshuram is a devout, orthodox Brahmin; he seeks, and obtains, that kind of power which will make the villagers follow his lead; he needs Kondura to convince the villagers, as underwriter of his claims to power; he needs the root to act as a divine constraint on, and guarantor of, his power and the actions which stem from it.

The spiritual and temporal power of Parshuram is underwritten by the sympathetic interpretation afforded it by his 'followers', the villagers. When the villagers ask Parshuram for advice on how to conduct their lives, on how to find meaning within them, Parshuram offers the platitudinous bromide of 'Surrender your will to God'. This is neither novel nor deep, yet the villagers respond as if an oracle had spoken. In describing his 'visions' of the Goddess, Parshuram says, 'She is not seen; she shows herself; you can see her in stones. It is up to her to be seen or not.' This deferment, a cloaking in mystery and ambiguity, is interpreted in the 'right way' by the villagers. Parshuram points at Anusuya – the Devi he sees in his visions – as he utters these words and the villagers take this as evidence of his greatness and humility: to acknowledge a woman, especially one's wife, as goddess, is saint-like! Besides his words, the villagers interpret concomitant physical phenomena and Parshuram's actions 'correctly' too. At the village temple, as prayers are performed and Parshuram meditates, a snake enters, causing panic. Parshuram is oblivious to the presence of the snake, who, unchallenged and undisturbed, continues his wanderings. This encounter, easily explainable in commonsensical naturalistic terms, triggers awe in the watching villagers, who, now conditioned to interpret Parshuram's actions and pronouncements in a divine light, regard this as proof of his divinity and fall at his feet. When the zamindar's family visits the temple, Parshuram is disturbed by a sexual fantasy involving Parvati while his devotees imagine his 'other-worldly' concentration undisturbed by the presence of wealthy people, who reduce others to offering obeisance to them. No matter what Parshuram's inner or outer state, it is interpreted 'appropriately' by his acolytes.

These phenomena, the water source predicted by the diviner, the 'tame snake', can be provided 'rational' explanations: no attempt had previously been made on the chosen plot of land to find water; it is Parshuram's determination to find water that keeps the workers working; the snake that does not bite Parshuram has not been trodden upon or disturbed; it has found its way into the temple space and wants to be left alone; the villagers move out of the snake's way while Parshuram remains sitting; the snake leaves him alone as it well might. But in the context of this interpretive space, in this charged perspective, these phenomena sustain Parshuram's vision and encourage him to continue in his 'enlightened' ways.

Parshuram's newly found powers are not uncontested: the village schoolmaster, the local voice of reason, who praises colonial authorities like the viceroy Lord William Bentinck for abolishing social pathologies like sati, which he describes as the violent coercion of a widow, remains sceptical and indeed, angrily critical of Parshuram's gnomic pronouncements and erratic behaviour; he wonders how Parshuram became susceptible to grandmothers' tall tales and myths. On hearing Parshuram say the Devi has commanded him to undertake the task of temple construction, the teacher, angered by this self-indulgent 'faith', says, 'Fulfil your actual duties. Don't build temples; teach children. Because of faith our country has suffered; we need fires in the peasant's home, not lamps in the temple.' The teacher stands outside sacred and temporal power, symbolizing reason, a force of rationality that urges scepticism and pragmatism upon primitive superstition; he, well aware of the power and potential of religious myth, especially in its interactions with a 'primed' audience like the villagers, wishes some social good would come of this superstition, that it not only be used as a testing ground for Kondura and as a further propping up of the power of organized religion and its earthly executors, the priest and the landlord.

In *Kondura*, Benegal returns to familiar themes of uprisings against feudal powers, the patriarchal conceptions of sexuality and the sexual exploitation of women. The landlord Bhairav Murthy's violent, rapacious, sexual exploitation of the peasant women, who are reconciled to their sexual slavery, shows that he is a rakshasa (demon) come down to earth, one described as the mythical demon king Ravana of the *Ramayana*. The potential uprising against him, even if backed by divine power, is contained, a failure, because the landlord transcends and overpowers the magical powers made available to Parshuram. This is a denial of the agency of the divine by the earthly powers of the human landlord; Parshuram's failure to understand the true source of the 'growing sin' underwrites his undermining by the deviousness of the landlord, who senses that the new saint, while claiming divine powers, is merely a man in his understanding of women. This notion is most dramatically demonstrated when a villager's wife is ordered to the zamindar's house to be his new sex slave, leaving her infant baby unattended. The baby will die of neglect and hunger; this is the progression of sin in the village 'the saint

Parshuram' does not notice, for he only has eyes for the transgression of conventional sexual propriety. As a Brahmin, he cannot 'see' the abuse of a class of people he has not seen fit to consider his equals in the past; his eyes are turned elsewhere, to the heavens, seeking divine visions. When the distraught father seeks comfort from the 'god-man', Parshuram merely offers him the consolation of seeking comfort through praying to the Goddess. At the landlord's estate, where Murthy violently assaults Vasu, Parvati vocally defends him while Parshuram offers no judgement; he is obsessed with placating divine power and ignores earthly pathology.

Benegal returns, too, to familiar feminist themes, present here in the unrequited sexuality of Anusuya, and in the resistance Parvati shows to the supposed saint-like qualities of Parshuram. In *Kondura*, the three dimensions of power are made manifest: sacred, temporal and sexual; the contestations between the three reveal the true complexity of their interactions with material realities. For it is in Parvati's responses to Parshuram that an exception to the worship of Parshuram by the villagers is found, as she sees through Parshuram's supposed saintliness to his thinly disguised sexual obsession with her, through his disdaining of earthly power to his ensconcement in the weekday. Parvati, as a woman subject to Parshuram's sexual desire, has seen through the facade; here again, if erotic love is an obsession not controlled by politics, it is, too, a force that cannot be disguised, least of all to the woman who is the subject of the erotic gaze, and can detect the cant with which the man seeks to obscure it. Parvati, the holder of sexual power, is well aware of its effect on sacred and profane power; if there is a goddess in the world Parshuram inhabits, she is to be found in Parvati, whose name identifies the divine feminine consort of Lord Shiva. Parvati insists Parshuram is a man, not a god; when her family touches his feet and asks for blessings Parvati declines. When Parshuram seeks to feed Parvati the divine root, she is suspicious, and wonders what sins she has committed to require such 'cleansing'. If the teacher represents conventional, empirical scepticism directed at Parshuram, Parvati's 'lack of faith' is corrosive and fatally undermining. As for Anusuya, the boon Parshuram is granted requires sexual denial by its beneficiary, but sexuality is not autonomous; to be celibate is to deny a sexual partner their sexuality. A woman may, too, become 'heroic' by sublimating herself and transcending her sexuality. But only if she chooses it freely; Parshuram's failure to realize this underwrites the destruction of his relationship with Anusuya. For Parshuram binds her with his commitment; he has spoken for her too. When he does seek her out, he does so in the guise of rape, a shattering betrayal that leads to Anusuya's suicide. His celibacy is chosen; hers is not; the result is tragic.

In showing how class and feudal power win out over the sacred and the divine and the magical and the mysterious, *Kondura* offers acute political commentary on the interplay of sacred and profane power and how the two might be transmuted into the other. We witness an opportunity to combat the power of the landlord with the power of myth and ritual, ancient forces that can be harnessed against new challenges. It is an emboldened Parshuram who can stride into the landlord's bedroom and demand an audience, an effrontery that could have led to instant expulsion and a flogging; but this subaltern, now possessed of a divine power, can take on earthly powers. Political subjects, as Benegal's realist commitments suggest, do not respond to abstract political theory; the moral universe they delineate requires the right kind of conceptual key to unlock it, one generated by their understanding of the forces that rule their lives. For the villagers in *Kondura*, it is neither reason nor science, nor the deliverance of the modern liberal state. Power, here, comes in two forms: that of the zamindar, and that of the gods and his local representatives. If the zamindar is God's representative, as he was originally, then obeisance is due him; if there is a new divine representative, then allegiance is transferred to him.

In *Kondura*, profane power is better acquainted with the particulars of the village; even divine power finds itself blunted and run aground when confronted with this precisely placed and aimed local temporal power. If Parshuram had had visions of overthrowing the landlord, of evicting him from his palace, he would have been supported by the villagers who had seen evidence of his magical powers and are ready to follow him; his power, acquired from his belief he was the beneficiary of a 'boon' from Kondura, allows him to overcome the local seat of power of the priest; it allows him to 'talk back' to both the zamindar and the priest, the holders of profane and sacral power. Closer to home, he can overcome his elder brother, a man who had previously only castigated, ridiculed and humiliated him. But his fatal lack of alliance with women, his lack of empathetic understanding of their desires and capacities, dooms this incipient revolution, rendering it stillborn.

Kondura is as much a metaphysical and epistemological document as it is a moral and political one as it seeks to answer the question of why profane power outsmarts the divine. *Kondura*'s answer: because of the lack of political imagination, a failure to believe wholly in the power granted to a revolutionary, in a full-bore commitment to political change, to finding new political allies. In politics, too, there are superstitions; patriarchy is an abiding human one.

Kalyug

'Classics' and 'great works' of literature 'endure through the ages' because their form and content illuminate and embody archetypal moral, social and cultural preoccupations. This is especially true of the great Indian epics, the *Ramayana* and the *Mahabharata*, which have provided rich grist for generations of Indian artists in the visual and literary arts – as they have for Benegal's directorial and storytelling mill. Such inspiration was evinced in *Ankur* and *Nishant*, which both drew on and 'rebooted' critical segments of these epics to make allegorical claims, to demonstrate their modernity, to offer a cinematic explanation of their longevity. For instance, Benegal condemns Surya's abandonment of Lakshmi in *Ankur* via a moral archetype derived from the *Ramayana* where the turning out of his pregnant wife, Sita, by Ram, is a crucial embarrassment in the greatest saint-king of all. And *Nishant* is plausibly understood as a 'rebooting' of a narratively crucial segment of the *Ramayana*, the abduction of Sita by the lustful Ravana, the demon king, in depicting the kidnapping of Sushila, the village teacher's wife, by the grasping feudal lords; in Benegal's rebooting, feudal power is shown to be the modern incarnation of demonic power, the modern-day Rama needs to have his masculinity shamed in order to exercise his kingly virtue, and the contemporary Sita's sexuality is a rather more complicated notion too.

This rich philosophical and artistic relationship continues in Benegal's *Kalyug* (The Age of Vice, 1981), 'a very bleak film'[17] that 'reboots' – offering an interpretation relevant to contemporary India's material and cultural being – the *Mahabharata* in modern India, featuring, like it, a bitter 'battle' between two factions of a family, not contesting a kingly inheritance but rather, engaged in competing manufacturing businesses. *Kalyug*'s allusive creation and posing of moral dilemmas within the constraints of familial demands and duties illustrates Benegal's claim that the *Mahabharata* finds its greatness in its perennially 'modern' refusal of impoverished dichotomies of 'totally evil or totally good'.[18] The *Mahabharata* relentlessly traffics in moral ambiguity, as in the tale of Eklavya, in which a lower-caste, forest-dwelling hunter gives up his pursuit of martial greatness in deference to a Brahmin teacher who wishes to assert the primacy of his princely student, or the killing of the aged teacher Dronacharya aided by a white lie told by the perennial truth-teller Yudhishthira. These tales introduce an uneasy dissonance in the *Mahabharata*'s readers who do not find within its pages an unambiguous delineation of the good and the bad; it is potentially revolutionary in its impact on conventional, 'precious', ethical and political ideals. *Kalyug* reclaims the subversion of the original epic, which gestured at the dark transactional heart of the Indian family, whose filial ties were disrupted by a kingly inheritance: murder, deception and greed were driven by desire for kingdom.

Such a reading, crucially, resists an interpretation of the *Mahabharata* as an ancient repository of Hindu moral wisdom in a sonorous Sanskritized idiom. During the 1990s, such an understanding of the great Indian epics was made the basis of a communal, public celebration of all things Hindu as the *Ramayana* and the *Mahabharata* were telecast, every Sunday morning, in the form of extended serials on Indian national television; these were supposedly acting to 'unite' a nation around its greatest cultural inheritance but at the implicit cost of discarding other historical contributions to the Indian mosaic, like Urdu poetry or Mughal architecture, or even a more complicated vision of 'Indian values' and 'the Indian sensibility'. By reclaiming the *Mahabharata* from the vanguard of a reactionary social revival, one that would use it to police and instruct, *Kalyug* makes the *Mahabharata* remind Indians that the human drama enacted here is one that connects it to the tapestry of human experience extending through time and space, in all places and all times. In doing so, *Kalyug* participates in the debate over what constitutes literature; *Kalyug*'s answer is that it is those texts that result in such philosophically fertile reinterpretations.

Kalyug is thus a tribute to, a celebration of, the *Mahabharata* in showing its continuing and enduring relevance for having established archetypes of fundamental human conflicts, and in supporting larger claims about the ambiguous historical relationship between material conditions and social consciousness. If the rural, agrarian, 'pre-modern' age of kings and princes and commoners were to produce the intrigue, skulduggery and murderous impulses visible in the *Mahabharata*'s many interwoven tales, then which sensibilities do the age of industrialization and commerce and the 'modern family' produce? *Kalyug*'s unflinching look at the world of corporate affairs supplies part of the answer, and it is not a reassuring one. *Kalyug* wears its moral ambiguity, or indeed its amorality, on its sleeve; the modernity it displays has not corresponded to an accompanying arc of moral improvement; the commodification of human sensibilities is all-pervasive, and the perdition on display is great.

In Indian mythology, 'kalyug' is the fourth stage of the world's cosmological and spiritual development and history, an age of 'strife', 'discord', 'quarrel' or 'contention', a signal the decline of the world has begun, to end in its destruction before the cycle of creation and destruction begins anew. *Kalyug* is a testament to the *Mahabharata*'s illustration of the political, ethical and cultural truths which produce such decay in the modern era. In particular, *Kalyug* is an indictment of the world of business, which claims the pursuit of moral ideals is an unprofitable enterprise betraying shareholder value and quarterly profit reports; the teaching of 'business ethics' in business schools and the appointment of token ethicists to corporate boards does little to combat the corrosions of moral sensibilities which are an inevitable by-product of early, industrial, or even late-stage capitalism. During the epic battle of Kurukshetra, the dreaded chakravyuh, a spiral battle formation, entrapped many warriors, including Arjun's brave young son, Abhimanyu; *Kalyug*'s narrative encloses such a structure for the families who are drawn, willingly or not, into the 'heart of darkness' of the pursuit of profit. None, not even the eventual 'victors', emerges unscathed.

Kalyug shows, like *Nishant* before it, that the unleashing of violence, especially that driven by the desire for vengeance and profit, is catastrophic and unpredictable, triggering ramifications that are uncontrollable: war is not planned glory; it is what we find ourselves fighting as we stumble through our rage and hubris. *Kalyug*'s 'war of the families' is not glorious; it is sordid and mean-spirited; there is 'friendly fire' and innocents die; conspiracies abound and lies are told; dirty secrets of past transgressions emerge; disgrace is in abundance.

In *Kalyug*, corporate life produces wealth for its characters, visible in landed estates, well-furnished homes, gambling, leisure games and expensive scotch whisky. Life is good, if material pleasures are its yardstick. But *Kalyug*'s characters are deeply unhappy and conflicted; their infrequent displays of joy only occur on commercial success and when their machinations and scheming bear fruit, even if at the considerable expense of their family members. For while this is a young and modern nation, at its heart lie greed and the oldest kinds of rivalries, familial discord and sexual jealousy. In *Kalyug*'s Freudian vision, while the nation's external wrappers change, the animating and growing 'inner culture' carries malignant traces of its past. All things – including the Indian family and its ideals – decay over time; *Kalyug* shows these have always enjoyed questionable claims for their moral sanctity. In the old days, the lure of kingly power drove cousins to murder; now, the pressures of the commodities and stock market and the manufacturing schedule do. *Kalyug* is a critique of modernization, of the corrosive and tragic corruption of human relationships, of the Indian family's ethical ideals by commerce and industry and capitalism – even as it suggests this is an old pathology reborn in a modern incarnation appropriate to its positioning in time and space.

The *Mahabharata* parcelled out the 'good' and the 'bad' into categories indexed by political valence and caste-based duties, thus disrupting their older boundaries; in *Kalyug*, the criterion for normative judgement and arbitration is 'business sense'. Its characters are equally seduced by power, equally corrupted and destroyed; their moral judgement is suspended while they perform economic calculations underwritten by rage and shame. Class distinctions do not enable us to distinguish between its characters for a trade unionist, the representative of the working class, is shown to be as manipulative and cynical as the figureheads of corporate middle-class ownership. The workers recede into insignificance; here there is no meaningful labour solidarity, industrial action is compromised, the strike is a cynical front for backstage conspiracy. In this political economy, all participants are tainted in its supposed 'moral' dimensions; sincerity gives way to nihilism.

Kalyug uses a complex family chart – a visual analogue of Indian epics' complicated familial and political interrelationships of their rich cast of characters – to introduce the 'warring' families and factions, the Khubchands and the Puranchands, headed by the patriarch Bhishanchand, the grandfather. The opening sequence, set on a factory floor with complex manufacturing processes underway, shows the modern symbols of economic and political power, the giant machines of industry which dwarf men, and which drive their affairs and fortunes and attenuate their moral trajectories. These factories are modern palaces, their boardrooms and conference chambers modern battlefields; the industrial and the commercial are the proving grounds of the ethical here; in these new battlefields is the modern Indian epic written.

Conflict and naked commercial ambition is the central theme in *Kalyug* as the Puranchands fail to secure a prestigious, high-value manufacturing contract, humiliatingly awarded instead to their cousins' rival manufacturing unit, and immediately seek to regain the economic and commercial advantage through a series of legal and formal manoeuvres resisted by the Khubchands. The Khubchands and Puranchands' scheming and counter-scheming to sabotage and compromise each other's manufacturing operations proceeds in defiance of their parents' words of caution and desire for irenic reconciliation; the older idealistic, sentimental India gives way to the younger, ruthless, ambitious India, driven by a desire for greater profit, even if at the cost of familial disruption. Despite various attempts to rein in actors and their deeds through revelations and warnings, the ageing parents can exert little control over their angry, vengeful and ambitious children and are reduced to the status of helpless bystanders as a tragic cycle of fatal plots and reprisals ensues, resulting in the deaths of Sandeep Khubchand (a stress-induced heart attack); Balraj Puranchand's son Sunil (an assassination attempt that takes out the wrong target); Karan Singh, the Khubchands' able lieutenant (murdered) and finally Dhanraj Khubchand (suicide). In *Kalyug*'s closing scenes, we pan back to a view of the city, the home of modern India. What further corruptions of the Indian ethical and spiritual ideal await in the city's factories and boardrooms? What do their balance sheets reveal in their adding up of profits and losses? Will these only be financial, or will they indicate other kinds of moral injuries sustained?

Benegal constructs his rebooting of the *Mahabharata* through parallelisms of plot and character of varying exactness. The Puranchand brothers (sons of the widowed Savitri) stand in for the Pandavas while the Khubchand brothers (ably assisted by Karan Singh) stand in for the Kauravas. The Puranchand's most interesting member is, in keeping with Benegal's commitment to strong women characters, the fiery, beautiful and stern Supriya, the eldest Puranchand brother Dharamraj's wife, an 'austere and brusque woman' who embodies knowledge, power, beauty and sexuality. Supriya stands in for the *Mahabharata*'s Draupadi, who, in Benegal's 'post-feminist' interpretation, rather than being 'used' by five husbands is 'woman enough' for five husbands.[19] Supriya embodies polyandrous and matriarchal power, and dominates conventional social situations; she is a strict mother, not given to frivolous displays of affection or maternal indulgence, impatient with womanly affection and softness. Benegal recreates, too, the *Mahabharata*'s infamous 'disrobing of Draupadi' episode, as prompted by a complaint from the Khubchands, income tax officers raid the Puranchand residence, and while searching their home, rifle through Supriya's undergarments. Like the Pandavas' ancestors, Dhritarashtra and Pandu, in the original epic, the Puranchands harbour the dark secret that they are 'bastards', sired by the holy man Swami Premchand, whom the Khubchands caustically describe as 'serviced' by Savitri, their aunt (married to the impotent Seth Puranchand). In the original epic, the replacement of a member of the warrior caste, unable to perform his 'breeding duties' because of his untimely death, by a virile member of the priestly caste was a profound reversal of the Indian caste order, a co-opting of the warrior's family by the 'heirs' of the sage.[20] Karan Singh, a sophisticated and solitary man, is Karna, that tragic character of the *Mahabharata* who was the Pandavas illegitimate half-brother, unknown to them; rejected and humiliated, for Draupadi had prevented Karan from seeking her hand in marriage, asserting her higher-caste privilege against the son of 'a mere charioteer', he became the Kauravas' most trusted lieutenant and warrior.

A fatal, morally significant, intervention in *Kalyug*'s grim downward spiral of violence is made by the ageing mother, Savitri, who asks for Karan's help in resolving the family's crisis and shocks him by telling him he is her son; indeed, the eldest of all, also sired by Swami Premchand, one she had disowned before her marriage. Savitri pleads to Karan he should be committed to helping her save her other sons, his younger brothers and now his economic rivals. This revelation, and Savitri's subsequent demand, torment and confuse Karan, raising the question of whether a mother can make such potent normative claims upon a son to whom she has never been a mother, whether in fact, such duties as she claims are his are even existent in any form. But this display of moral and spiritual angst on Karan's part, and his subsequent frantic attempts to rein in the violence underway show it is Karan alone who acquires a conscience in *Kalyug* as he notes with growing alarm the unimpeded moral decline of those around him. From Karan's perch, where the greatest deprivation is emotional, the absence of a home and his parents, the squabbling of the cousins is a battle among the privileged. This 'homeless' man finds the possibility to forswear the demands of the commercial and the economic for the familial; he seeks to draw back, but the central tragedy of *Kalyug* is that he is too far drawn in, too deeply implicated, to save himself literally and figuratively.[21]

By setting the *Mahabharata* in a 'new India', Benegal suggests the 'old India' persists with all its moral ambiguities, that using the *Mahabharata* for conventional moral instruction, as a repository of 'traditional Indian moral wisdom', elides the depth, complexity and ambiguity of the original text, which accommodates interpretations of widely differing 'moral lessons'. *Kalyug* reiterates Rajmohan Gandhi's claim India is not a peaceful or a non-violent culture, that violence is part of the Indian ethos; its central epics are stories of war featuring intrigues and machinations, like those witnessed in *Kalyug*. It is unsurprising, Benegal suggests, that a culture which places war at such an apex cultural point, which suggests war is the warrior's moral duty even if at the cost of killing kith and kin, should give rise to a 'combative commercial ideal' as well, one that traffics freely in the commodified relationship and the cheapened ethical ideal.

The Puranchand and Khubchand families' degradation in *Kalyug* is visible not just in their cynical decline into violence but also in the sexual shaming of Savitri, the ageing mother, by the Khubchands who invite the sage, her erstwhile 'lover', Swami Premchand, to a family celebration; the family's moral downfall has found a familiar form of expression. Shaming women for their sexual desire is the oldest patriarchal trick of all; there is no condemnation directed at the Swami, a supposed 'holy man' committed to a vow of chastity. At *Kalyug*'s conclusion, when Savitri informs her sons that Karan, the man they successfully schemed to murder, was their eldest brother, a distraught Bharat screams '*kulta!*' (whore) and moves to assault her but is held back by his brothers. Bharat conveys, violently, his disapproval of his mother's lack of 'sexual purity'. Bharat knows he has killed his brother; he is the modern Oedipus, driven into fratricidal violence because of fatal ignorance. His father is not the one he imagined; his birth was illicit; these radical changes in his understandings of himself cause a new self to split off from the older, one willing to abuse this frail woman who has brought his older world crashing down around him. Bharat collapses and is comforted by Supriya, who calls for the door to be locked behind her and tenderly strokes his face and forehead, reassuring him she will take care of him; their ambiguous relationship is destined to continue in their attenuated family. This 'new mother', one known to be not sexually innocent, has been found for this man-child. Such are the consolations required by those kept too busy by the demands of commerce to tend to their souls.

A blundering escalation of hostilities, driven along by hubris, anger and misunderstanding, by old emotions, repressed and hidden in the familial unconscious, produces *Kalyug*'s central tragedies. The great culminating battle of the *Mahabharata* resulted in an ambiguous victory for the Pandavas; *Kalyug*'s war is as exacting. *Kalyug* is a sustained critique of capitalism's corrosion of filial and commercial relationships: the Puranchands' and the Khubchands' workers, like the dumb, unnamed soldiers who fought the battle of Kurukshetra, are pawns. These workers do not fight for their rights; they are reduced to being manipulated by their masters, by their own economic constraints. Here, we find Marcuse's 'unification of opposites'[22] as negotiations between 'labour' and 'management' are farcical conspiracies and collusions.

Kalyug functions, vividly, as a record of cultural, moral and political decadence. The older *Mahabharata* spoke of kingly inheritances and battles and invoked the 'glorious' rhetoric of warfare. The new one is considerably removed from such glory; the arc of historical and moral development on view is one of decline. If the *Mahabharata* were to be written today, *Kalyug*'s world of corporate business would be its logical setting, its workers and managers and accountants its plausible characters.

Trikaal

Trikaal (Past, Present, and Future, or, Three Eras, 1985) is a homage to an older way of life, a historical document recording cultures in transition, set in the tiny, tropical, 'beach-and-church' state of Goa at the time of its 'liberation' by Indian armed forces in 1961. Its central and most important characters are women; indeed, the movie begins with the death of a patriarch, Senor Suarez, the domineering, lusty head of an Indo-Portuguese family, and finds its most vivid conflicts in the contestations among its women characters, his wife Dona, his daughter Sylvia and his granddaughters, Aurora and Anna. Though its narrator is a man, we feel and sense its inquiring and critical gaze shift to direction by the central women characters. Within *Trikaal*, eras and epochs mingle and interact: seances evoke a misremembered past; some characters want to hurry on to the future, freeing themselves from present constraints; others cling to the past, seeking its ambiguous comforts; yet others, living or not, emerge from the past to haunt the present. As the characters converse and ruminate on their present embroilments, a larger material reality intrudes in the form of the Indian Army preparing to invade Goa – as it did in 1961 to summarily evict its Portuguese garrison, an archaic colonial holdover, which had failed to notice the eviction of the British Empire, the creation of the nation of India and its new postcolonial polity.[23] *Trikaal*'s depiction of these intermingling periods, and of the blend of spiritual, political and moral that results, offers acute metaphysical and existential commentary in a story about mourning, losses of many kinds, picking up the pieces to construct a new world, and finding new meanings in their collection and assemblage, all the while making connections between moments in time and space that are underwritten by capricious, self-centred and purposeful memory.

Trikaal is shot as a sustained flashback 'generated' by the narrator Ruiz Pereira (Naseeruddin Shah) who returns for a visit to his older Goan home after twenty-four years. To return 'home' requires a new physical route, a novel psychic path, too, back to historical recesses of individual and group memory and the partially remembered past. As Ruiz is driven through Goa, he muses,[24]

> I am returning after 24 years; I left before liberation. No one will remember me; but I remember everything. My village is like a Ming dynasty bouquet. If you do not understand its history, its story, it will only look like a beautiful, delicate bunch of flowers. Its culture will fade away, like old memories. My personal vase is this abandoned old mansion. The Suarez family lived here for 350 years.

The Suarez family is the centrepiece of *Trikaal*, beginning with the funeral of the patriarch Erasmo, a philandering, lusty landlord drawn straight from a Gabriel Garcia Marquez novel, and culminating in the dissolution of the family; much as Suarez is dispersed into the cosmic 'four elements' following his death, the Suarez family is reduced to elemental form and must find new homes for repose. In *Trikaal* 'magical realism'[25] produces a 'wider' and 'extended' reality,[26] suggesting a naturalistic world order cannot do justice to our lived experience: Senor Suarez's material existence is over, but his continued presence in Dona Maria's life shows his 'psychosocial dimension' lives on.[27] For in the aftermath of Senor Suarez's death, Senora Suarez, Dona Maria (Leela Naidu) refuses to accept the truth of its occurrence, indulging in fado recitals in her chambers, disdaining the organization of her husband's funeral and the betrothal of her beautiful granddaughter Anna to the woebegone Erasmo, visiting from Lisbon with his parents. Sylvia, for her part, is irate at these displays of her mother's mysterious reluctance to face up to 'reality'; she is possessed of an acute anxiety at the thought her daughter might lose this 'good match'. These delays are eased, but along the way, Goa falls to India, Anna becomes scandalously pregnant, ghosts of all kinds make appearances and secrets from the past find traction in the present. Our narrator terminates his story where he, having generated sexual scandal himself, is summarily 'exiled' and begins his journey to the 'great wide world outside'.

Trikaal offers a sustained investigation of time, a natural subject for Benegal, an imagist and montagist whose temporal effects and intercutting techniques displace events and enable such rumination. This 'playing with time' in a visual and artistic medium in time provokes inquiry into, and introspection about, the role the past and future, remembered and anticipated, play in our present. With all three epochs folded into *Trikaal* we are offered a claim about their simultaneous coexistence and influence in our lives, which stand revealed as the nexus of our pasts and futures. In *Trikaal*, the past lives on, most vividly, in the language spoken by the Portuguese community and in the political crisis enveloping the Suarez family; it lives on in the reconfigured lives of those left behind in their mourning; the future of an independent, postcolonial India, a world dimly visible, exists in the present as potentiality, driving and directing the actions of the living, configuring and resolving present crises. The future is not mere dormant possibility, inertly waiting our presence; rather it is active, propelling us onwards by its insistent demands for realization and instantiation.

The opening scenes of *Trikaal* roll up the past into the present as we see a coffin brought to the Suarez home for Senor Suarez's corpse, and a cab bringing Ruiz Pereira back to his older home in the present; these shots' lack of co-temporality is not immediately manifest. A man carrying a coffin walks through a lush green field; a car drives along a road; a grave is dug in a graveyard; the coffin bearer enters the Suarez home. This sequence is imposed by observers; time is, as Aristotle noted, the sequencing of events. *Trikaal* acknowledges our understanding of time is subjective and relative to an imposed order, playing with which imposes alternative causalities, reversing established schemata of moral comprehension and blame.

Trikaal suggests the past cannot be conveniently forgotten, that archaic trauma repressed and banished is trauma selected to play a continuing role in the present. Dona Maria is unwilling to let her dead husband 'pass on', reluctant to abandon Ernesto, literally and figuratively: 'If I forget his face, I'll forget mine. All we will have left is memories.' These gnomic pronouncements continue at the funeral repast:[28]

> Who knows what the future will bring, we can only marry it with the past, only the past is alive. It goads us, tempts us to change it,

to relive it, but you only want to forget the past. That is why you are wandering on unknown paths.

Dona remains lost in her reveries, seeking her husband at seances conducted through the voice of Melagrenia, Erasmo's illegitimate child, now a faithful maid. But when Dona – reluctant to observe the changing of the guard at home, the transition in power – invokes Ernesto to preserve older memories and ways of being, the spectre of Vijay Singh Rane, a rebel against Portuguese rule, and one betrayed by the collaborating Suarezes to the Portuguese colonial administration, appears. We learn that Dona Maria has elided her family's history of collaborationist violence, a shameful act of colonial abnegation; ironically, the woman who reveres the past suffers from historical amnesia; her Freudian memory is selective. The past 'has a mind of its own': despite Dona's commands to leave, Rane insists on providing reminders of her family's complicity and guilt:[29]

> Your grandfather beheaded me for the governor. My screams filled the house, my blood soaked the cellar. Your grandfather murdered me; I was innocent. I didn't die happy. You betrayed me. I was of this land. Why was I given to the Portuguese? Your grandfather did not show mercy to my lover. You snatched our names and erased our identities. The foundation of this house is built on quashed hopes. Your family worked with the Inquisition.

The faces of the past victims of colonial rule that appear to Dona Maria in these visitations are the faces of those, who, like the family priest, still live on, suggesting the eternal recurrence and reincarnation of souls and archetypes, especially those which bear trauma and demand 'healing' and resolution by the present.

Dona Maria's seeming comfort with the past is thus ambiguous, for she only desires her desired selection of it, seeking to move on from the colonial guilt the ghosts of Rane want to revisit on her, to hide evidence of her family's collaboration with the colonial oppressors, their implication in the terrible Inquisition in Goa. (A moral catastrophe that fails to receive adequate historical attention and remembrance in modern India; Dona Maria's selective memory is also that of India's which swept these historical atrocities under the rug as it moved on to nationhood.) But memories, unwanted and wanted come rushing back in, unbidden and unwelcome, unceremoniously demanding a reckoning with. These mentions of the colonial past show this present placid scene is underwritten by considerable violence: the blood of those tortured during the Goa Inquisition or those hunted down as enemies of the colonial regimes soaks this land, unwilling to be denatured out of present nostalgic remembrances.

Trikaal's atmosphere is of an intimate chamber drama, set in dark interiors with low lighting, where conversations take place in corners and crannies; as befitting a 'ghost story', a Goan Gothic tale, *Trikaal* offers an acute visual interplay of darkness and light and revelation. In the dimly lit interiors of the Suarez residence, it is ghosts that provide illumination, forcing an inspection of the nooks and recesses of memory that have been kept hidden over the years.

In *Trikaal*, reality is porous as spirits come and go; there is no insistence on a sharp dividing line between the realm of the real and the supposedly non-existent. Dona's seances, the junction of the supernatural and the empirical, provoke the ire of 'official religion', which takes such transgressions on its domain of the spiritual and the immaterial very seriously. The family priest's warning to Dona Maria she should not interfere with the workings of the spirits during her seances is not issued in a spirit of mockery or ridicule; it is understood that humans can intervene in the supernatural. Conversely, the ghosts Dona Maria invokes are not frivolous; they have a political and moral agenda, for the immateriality of the spirit world is not without influence in this spatiotemporal physical world; at the very least, the colonial past demands that modern India acknowledge its new citizens will include former collaborators with inquisitionists and imperialists.

Trikaal, like *Kondura* before it, claims the supernatural, understood as not-existent in the naturalistic world view, is not a realm available for naturalistic inspection and analysis but instead emerges at the interplay of an intense emotional expression: personal crises trigger these invocations of, and encounters with, the supernatural. The suggestion the natural order of the world is disturbed by the intense emotional states of a supplicant hearkens back – as it did in *Kondura* – to the Hindu mythological theme of intense meditation securing an audience with the gods. Reality then, is not a distant order of Being resistant to our imprecations, rather it is actively shaped by our emotional interactions with it: the nature of the inquirer affects the nature and the content of the inquiry; the 'form of being' depends on the nature of the inquiry and the inquirer. Here, metaphysics and epistemology merge, for those who 'believe' inhabit different orders of being from those who do not.

Trikaal's other obsessions centre on identity and belonging, for none of its characters appear to have spiritual or physical homes in time or space. Their ostensible home, Goa, does not have a secure home in India; the young Anna is reluctant to be 'banished' to a new home; the Portuguese community refuses to accept their time in India, guarding an enclave in a postcolonial land, is at an end. Some characters assert Goans are not Indians but Portuguese citizens, others assert independence from Portugal, while yet others wonder if Goan independence is only for the 'landed'. Dona Maria is suspended between earthly and heavenly realms; Sylvia in waiting for the betrothal of her daughter; Leon, Anna's former lover, escapes from a Portuguese prison, sent there because he sought to liberate his home, Goa, from colonial rule, and promptly scurries into a bowel of the Suarez home, there to 'haunt' the family further, for he is soon reunited with Anna with momentous consequences, making her pregnant. The Indo-Portuguese, caught between two cultures, are despised by the Portuguese for not being sufficiently white or Portuguese and despised by Indians for their Otherness, for not being 'Indian enough'. Ironically, with *Trikaal*, Benegal was 'accused' of making 'a foreign film' even as he sought to make a movie about the richness and complexity of Indian identity, its history of being informed by both the 'local' and the 'imported'. *Trikaal* shows the Indian nation is far more diverse and fragmented than imagined with ambiguous loyalties to it; within a land imagined home many homeless roam, their homes not adequately defined by physical location, family ties, or national and religious allegiance. *Trikaal* suggests nationalist discourse, a supposedly unifying force, may be the great silencer of a diversity of voices, struggling to find expression for an ambiguous and ambivalent sense of belonging and identity. (*Trikaal* extends a homage to the Goan community's history, traditions and cultural inheritance; this includes, unsurprisingly for a Benegal production, a soundtrack featuring contemporary Goan artistes.)

Benegal returns in *Trikaal* to familiar themes of Indian class and caste relationships. The Catholic Suarez family, in distinctively Indian fashion,[30] speak incessantly of their own caste and refuse marriages to those outside their caste, including one to a proposal that would rescue their honour. Dona Maria maintains Ruiz Pereira cannot marry her pregnant granddaughter because he is not of the same caste as them; Dona would rather be humiliated by an illegitimate child than by an out-of-caste marriage. Benegal indicts the feudal, too, for such is the Suarez home: Melagrenia's servant body is available for use by all. Dona's encounter with the supernatural is marked by the exploitation of Melagrenia as a medium; when Melagrenia becomes pregnant, the seances come to a halt. The young Ruiz Pereira makes Melagrenia pregnant, but he has no desire to father the child, marry

Melagrenia or have any relationship with her besides the carnal. Ruiz is a callow and insensitive young philanderer who exploits the bodies of the women who work for his class; even as he serenades Anna with songs of love, he launches a series of uninvited forays on Melagrenia to claim his 'dues'. (In this dimension, there is a straightforward continuity between the Surya of *Ankur*, the Vishwam of *Nishant* and the Ruiz of *Trikaal*; each 'landed' man uses, and moves on from, the body of a disempowered woman.) In the Suarez kitchen, the servants, speaking in subaltern tones of resentment and resignation, speak of their hatred for their former master and how their lives will not change if their new masters – the approaching Indian forces – take over. The basement and kitchen, the private in this public, are unaffected by its great changes; here, the same power regimes will continue. Perhaps postcolonial nationalism is an affectation that will do little to ease the travails of the subalterns who must be co-opted into the national project.

Its many and various invocations of the interplay of memory, trauma, time, repression and resistance make *Trikaal* the most psychoanalytic of Benegal's movies; as in *The Seventh Horse*, the narrator, Ruiz Pereira, does not offer merely an exculpation but also a condemnation of his past. *Trikaal* raises several related questions: What is Ruiz seeking to accomplish by the recounting of this story? Why dredge up these memories if not to act upon them? Why these memories, and not others? Why are these events so important, so formative, for a grown man with contemporary loves and preoccupations? Ruiz himself questions his motives for returning:

> Did I return because of Melagrenia? Poor, dumb one, treated like a milk cow, back then she meant nothing, even now, perhaps, lost in the ocean, turned into a memory. How long can guilt torment us? It will become a memory too like all others.

Melagrenia was not Ruiz's greatest love; he does not miss their child and has not come to establish the bonds of fatherhood. Even as he speculates about Melagrenia, he does not bother to look too far or further for her and writes off her memory as he leaves, acknowledging that even this ruefulness will pass into time. At best, Ruiz can offer a partial confession of shame and regret. Is Ruiz reminding us of a time when he could make sexual conquests? Is a tale of 'dashing romantic failure' better than a recounting of staid domesticity and professional success? Perhaps the recounting of this tale allows Ruiz some measure of completion in his understanding of himself; his memories offer ample opportunity to understand himself through the lenses of caste, religion, gender and nationality, through inclusion in a national history, an entry in an imaginary Journal of Goan Liberation. Perhaps Ruiz is India, which must not forget its Goan past, and must integrate its memories, bad and good, into its conceptions of itself. Like Dona Maria, it must acknowledge the moral crimes committed in its name, the diversities it wrote out of existence and into its unity.

The memories of the Suarez family, like the Suarezes themselves, will fade away; nations, like Portugal and India, will come and go, and the human drama will find new form and expression in new people and new nations. *Trikaal* suggests that those novel entities, like us, should look around carefully, for traces of the past and the future to 'work through' past repression and resistance, despite visitation by trauma or the memory of sin; this 'integration' is a task for individuals and nations alike. Benegal's contribution to this 'national work' in India is to have made a movie that expands the notion of India by paying homage to both a 'gone and forgotten' way of life and to a people whose signatures live on in the Indian present and drive the nation towards its undetermined and unrealized future.

Conclusion

As works of philosophy, Shyam Benegal's movies are distinctly Indian and yet articulate human perplexities in accessible and universalist idioms; they argue through their characters, their lives, their actions, their words. Their central function, very often, is to display and articulate implicit or explicit acts of political and personal resistance in the face of systematic social oppression. Benegal's rich, detailed, cinematic conceptions of political and moral contestation, which oppose 'mainstream cinema' and its 'status quo' values,[1] identify him as a political realist, a philosopher of culture and a serious moralizer. His self-avowed identity as 'Indian filmmaker', not 'abstract practitioner of the cinematic arts', places his politics, cultural critique and moralizing in a specific context, the Indian. Benegal does not graft 'external' politics and aesthetics into Indian cultural spaces; his work describes and prescribes 'organic' politics, an artistic commitment that adds to the persuasiveness and plausibility of his realist political 'prescriptions'. His critiques of social orders are not corrosive; within the bleak outlines of social dysfunction resistance and questioning embodied in strong, interesting characters indicate paths to a new social order; his movies exercise political optimism and hope, avoiding facile despair and nihilism even when political and moral pathology appear to demand them in response.

Benegal's relationship to realism, 'factuality' and empirical approaches to cinema are ironically manifest in his rejection of documentary cinema which is confined to 'observable phenomena'.[2] For Benegal, within the permissiveness of feature films, a director may be 'interpreting . . . exploring . . . re-shaping material', in a manner not permissible in the documentary's conventional 'obligation to factuality'.[3] Benegal is thus committed to a form of perspectivism, for the feature film entails the pursuit of a 'very subjective' truth;[4] facts arise *within* subjectivities and their perspectives. In particular, Benegal relies on the multiplicities of perspectives arising from the Indian cultural locations of caste, gender and class to express the 'simple and profound' complexity of social and political phenomena; in each case, sympathetic yet critical notes are struck.[5] His movie made, a cinematic thesis realized, Benegal is content to let his works acquire constructed meanings through further interpretive dialogue with the changing community of Indian and international viewers who find renewed political visions in them as India changes. The richness of the cinematic 'texts' Benegal provides – thanks to their multimodal integration of literary scripts, classical music and dance, and complex characters and politics – facilitates a dynamic hermeneutics, guaranteeing his works a longevity and cultural and political relevance in the face of the empirical realities of a dynamic polity like India's.

Benegal's cinema is resolutely feminist in its preoccupations and concerns because men, masculinity and patriarchy do not define normalcy in his movies; women are *present* and *visible* to challenge their conceptions and understandings of the shared world they inhabit. Women do not merely embroider men's lives and stories in Benegal's works; they are essential components of the philosophical and cultural spectacle on display. Benegal's movies accept the claim that 'woman . . . is a product elaborated by civilization' with her self determined 'through the action of others'. To understand woman then, we must view how she is 'made'; Benegal's resultant cinema of the personal documents women's micro- and macro-personal interactions in patriarchal society to show the 'most powerful mechanisms of women's oppression', the workings of family and marriage, giant pillars of Indian culture and society and politics and morality, are not 'exceptional singularities' but weekday exercises; a 'kitchen-sink' movie which exposes their internal dysfunction is as grand a political document as a formal academic treatise.

Benegal's directorial career began with the lens turned resolutely towards the rural, and the small town, well away from urban precincts, to provide cinematic depictions of patriarchy that are not a mere documentary record; rather, they are the *evidence* contained in a charge sheet against patriarchy – they expose its workings in the most intimate of spaces. By depicting and documenting oppression, by making the invisible visible, they accept the feminist responsibility to articulate the dimensions of women's oppression. Such description, sympathetic and curious, is a philosophical statement all its own, in revealing to us hitherto hidden premises and possible rhetorical manoeuvres for future political arguments.

Benegal's central focus is the Indian family, Indian patriarchy's central institution, which acting as a mediator between public and private, enforces its 'control and conformity'[6] through particularly Indian forces that oppress women and restrain their personal and psychosocial development. Benegal's cinema shows such enforcement proceeds via private and public, sacred and secular, sanctions; these act to discipline and punish those who transgress, reminding those watching and listening of the penalties for non-compliance. His works depict patriarchy's agents – fathers, husbands, employers, landlords – forcing women to conform to its strictures, through 'institutional, interpersonal, and unconscious' sexism and the oppression engendered by 'exploitation, marginality, powerlessness . . . and violence'.[7] (An acute demonstration of the calculus of domestic patriarchy – which demands that one woman can only be empowered at the cost of another – is evinced in *Nishant* when Vishwam grants Sushila a measure of humanity in supporting her demands for a separate kitchen; in response, Rukmini complains Vishwam has given Sushila a 'wife's privileges', an ironic commentary on the 'imprisoned' status and sexual servitude of Indian wives.) Benegal shows oppression by men, whether high-caste landlords, lower-caste or middle-class, is systemic and structural, part of an unquestioned and 'natural' social fabric, a social and cultural context of 'forces and barriers' restraining, immobilizing and dehumanizing women.[8] It is this oppression, aided and abetted by a patriarchal ideology, which defines the 'normal' for Indian women. But this 'normal' is not an unquestioned or unchallenged one, and the agents of such questioning and challenge, Benegal claims and demonstrates, are the women themselves, not external saviours sent on from high. Indeed, in *Mandi*, when an 'external' woman saviour attempts to 'help' her 'sisters' we find she functions instead as an oppressive instrument of the patriarchal society she claims to be combating.

Benegal's movies ground their feminist claims in the quotidian, weekday acts of resistance by women in the private sphere, not systematic, organized, political 'movements' in the public sphere. There, women enact various modes of resistance in their sexual politics, 'power-structured relationships'[9] that socialize the sexes to the fundamentals of patriarchal politics in their weekday lives; their daily acts offer contestation and negotiation. These women are not 'brainwashed, moronised, robotised, lobotomised'[10] by patriarchy into being mere victims, their selves not 'so "invaded" by patriarchal conditioning' that they became 'non-persons';[11] instead, we see minor and major rebellions staged by women against structural arrangements that oppress them.

Indeed, this cinema's women persistently act to 'take the feet off their necks'.[12] In *Ankur*, Lakshmi's anger liberates her from Surya; he will never touch her again, and, indeed, finds his feudal power fatally compromised; in *Manthan*, Bindu chooses membership in the cooperative society after Rao's departure, in the company of another Harijan; the glimpse of the 'promised land' proves alluring enough to provoke political action; in *Nishant*, Sushila's sexual awakening resists the conventional understanding of Indian women's sexuality; in *Bhumika*, Usha refuses to be confined by the relationships patriarchal society offers her; in *Mandi*, Rukmini Bai is determined to live life on her own terms regardless of the social scorn directed at her; in *Junoon*, Ruth refuses to let colonialism or maternal authority confine her love; in *Trikaal* women display matriarchal power and make bold sexual choices; in *Kondura*, Parvati is the earthly, inquiring, sceptical, feminine counterpart to the arrogant, superstitious powers of the male; in *Kalyug*, Supriya's quiet, firm strength offers a dramatic contrast to the histrionics of her male counterparts; in *Suraj Ka Satwan Ghoda*, the women are never apologetic about their desires, whether economic or sexual. (Elsewhere Benegal shows other subalterns who resist or speak up: the stone-throwing child in *Ankur*, the peasants who revolt in *Nishant*, the Harijans who 'organize' and 'unionize' in *Manthan*, the mutineers in *Junoon*, the insolent prophet and his village followers in *Kondura*. In *Manthan*, Bindu and Bhola are ostensibly condemned to a life on the margins, to remaining utterly powerless and voiceless, but both speak, and loudly; they are not shy in seeking substantive personal and political change; Bhola is keen and eager to learn to read, to rise above his station in life; Bindu, in seeking a new love, seeks a new life; all while endangering themselves and the little they have zealously guarded; far more important for them is self-respect.)

Benegal shows, too, women who have made peace with patriarchy through collaboration and acquiescence. The depiction of women collaborators who have internalized feudal and patriarchal structures – like Porchamma in *Nishant*, Saru in *Ankur*, Shanti Devi in *Mandi* – confirms class and caste loyalty dominate their politics: women of privileged classes and castes find closer ties with men of their classes and castes than with the women of lower ones in some wholly imagined, non-existent 'womanly' solidarity. In *Nishant*, the servant woman Porchamma, unable to resist the landlord's power, has 'gone over', seeking to ensure she is on the right side of its dispensations. When Sushila wishes the door to her room closed, her futility in erecting a barrier against further assaults is vindictively and spitefully emphasized by Porchamma:

> Why do you lock the doors? The house is theirs. Where will you go? Your man will not accept you; your name is not spoken in the village; your husband will not accept you and will marry again.

This is a perfect prison, with fear, submission and collaboration as its fetters. Its guards include those who have made it home and accepted its impress of power upon themselves. Benegal thus demonstrates that the gender of Indian women cannot be separated from its production and maintenance by class and caste (and indeed, religion), thus lending his political claims their firm intersectional grounding and location. In *Nishant*, when Sushila reconciles herself to her captivity she slips into higher-caste roles as she asks to go to the temple in a car; as a mark of her 'settling down', she demands a separate kitchen, 'I'm going to live here as a proper woman and not a whore.' Significantly, her strongest claim to 'respectability' is her caste status, which enables the maintenance of a semblance of 'normalcy'. Mammo, an urban Muslim woman, is separated physically by the urban–rural divide, and psychically by the caste-class-religion divide, from Lakshmi and

Bindu, low-caste Hindu women; these varied women are, however, united by the diversity of patriarchal forms.

Patriarchy finds in India, its own particular cultural manifestations, producing a distinctive 'Indian gender of the feminine', in which a woman, otherwise disempowered, can find a safe haven by virtue of favourable location in caste, religion or class hierarchies; Indian women, Benegal's characters, deconstruct it through their existential decisions, by their public displays of their private politics. Benegal's realist aesthetic is therefore engaged in the *descriptive* project of gender, developing 'more accurate concepts through' the 'empirical or quasi-empirical method'[13] of a realist, highly specific cinema that seeks out particularities and distinctions in women's experiences of patriarchy. Benegal's movies offer a *positive* vision of liberation for Indian women which demands substantive political and social equality in social and political goods compared to women elsewhere *and* a differential and equitable evaluation of their femininity; Benegal aids in the project to 'redefine and revalue' gender by 'reconsidering its relationship with "race, nation, ethnicity and class"',[14] a theoretical demand long made on liberal feminism and one which can only be realized by the inclusion of women's lives, voices and politics from 'elsewhere'.

Benegal's work, importantly, aids the project of constructing a feminist conception of autonomy through accounts of women's resistance within cultures *and* their nurturing of relationships in the same spaces – his cinema aids in the construal of autonomy in 'social, relational, interpersonal, or intersubjective terms'.[15] A clichéd feminist heroine rejects her private sphere utterly; more morally and politically complex is the woman who 'stays on' to negotiate a more conducive space for herself, one founded on rearticulated relations of power with the representatives of patriarchy. The women in *Ankur*, *Manthan*, *Bhumika*, *Mandi*, *Trikaal*, *Sardari Begum* and

Junoon possess 'masculine' traits of 'strength' and 'independence' but remain enmeshed in a web of relationships of care. These women find purpose and meaning in their lives by the personal and emotional affiliations they build, maintain and, often, defend. In *Bhumika*, Usha is forced to become a social and relational atom; Benegal thus suggests patriarchy is morally corrosive in forcing an abandonment of care to more self-centred modes of being. The women in Benegal's movies know their independence and autonomy bring them censure from patriarchal society,[16] but their words and actions reinforce the subversive claim that no social institution is sacrosanct; some, such as marriage or traditional motherhood, which are 'infected' by the oppression of women, must give way especially when 'liberation' is not the abandonment of the family or personal relationships but a reconfiguration of their personal parameters, not a retreat to atomicity but an advance to a richer, respectful web of relationships.[17]

Benegal's work shows a profound consequence of structural sexism and patriarchy is men who are ignorant of, and disdain knowledge about, women; such men remain uncaring about their partners and their children, their moral orders impervious to a crucial knowledge. The absent father in *Mammo* is ignorant of his son and his life; Surya in *Ankur* is ignorant of Lakshmi's true motivations in sleeping with him; he remains convinced he has seduced her, that his sexual power is dominant; the men in *Bhumika* are ignorant of Usha's needs; Ruiz Pereira in *Trikaal* does not care to acquire knowledge about the fate of his child, borne by Melagrenia. In these depictions of the always-fraught relationships between men and women, Benegal does not merely valorize women's lives within patriarchy; he actively provides an illustration of how men morally corrode themselves by partaking of patriarchy's ill-gotten sins: it cheats men of an authentic sexuality or moral sense of themselves. They live, instead, in worlds of delusion, masters of a domain populated by those who resent and seek to subvert their dominion. Victories here can only be Pyrrhic.

Benegal's movies contain a vision of what a just world for women – one 'without gender'[18] – might look like; in this alternative world, a reimagining of our current one, its empowered women will resemble his women characters, 'fully recognized as free and equal persons'. Because this world is not yet realized, 'the process of reimagining ourselves'[19] continues in a cinema whose refusal to posit end points for our moral development enhances our political imagination. In writing of the interplay of words and violence, Martha Minow wrote, 'Are there words that can illuminate the universal in the particular and the particular in the universal? Talking differently, by itself, will not make things different. But unless we talk differently, we may never make things different.'[20] Movies enable us to talk differently; they supply us with a new language to do philosophy, and in Benegal's cinema, a highly ethical politics. Benegal's work finds its liberatory potential in showing the relations woman bears to man are limiting, not fully expressive of her being, destructive to her freedom and authentic sense of self; the clarity of his philosophical vision is evident in the glimpses of the new worlds he makes possible. Abstract theorizing cannot do this; it requires the vivid illustration and concreteness of Benegal's deeply moral cinema, his sympathetic and empathetic vision as philosopher and filmmaker.

Notes

Introduction

1 Sangeeta Datta, *Shyam Benegal* (New Delhi: Rolli Books, 2005), 211.

2 William van der Heide, *Bollywood Babylon: Interviews with Shyam Benegal* (New York: Bloomsbury, 2006), 24–7.

3 Benegal's work as a prolific and accomplished director of commercial advertisements granted him a familiarity with the 'pop grammar' of the cinematic or televised advertisement.

4 Pradip Krishen, 'Knocking at the Doors of Public Culture: India's Parallel Cinema', *Public Culture* 4, no. 1 (1991): 24–41, 34–5.

5 Robert Cross, 'Shyam Benegal's Ankur and the Nehruvian Woman', *Doshisha Studies in Language and Culture* 13, no. 2 (2010): 89–115, 91.

6 I owe these observations (and the quoted sentence), not explicitly made in an earlier draft of the manuscript, to an anonymous reviewer.

7 Costica Bradatan, 'Philosophy Has a Lot to Learn from Film', https://aeon.co/ideas/philosophers-have-much-to-learn-from-the-great-filmmakers (accessed November 2019).

8 Bryan Magee, *Confessions of a Philosopher* (New York: Random House, 1997), 399–400. Emphasis in original.

9 Raymond Geuss, *Philosophy and Real Politics* (Princeton: Princeton University Press, 2008).

10 Bradatan, citing Stephen Mulhall, *On Film* (New York: Routledge, 2001).

11 Hannah Arendt, 'Thinking: Appearance and Semblance', in *The Life of the Mind*, vol. I (New York: Harvest/HBJ, 1981).

12 Datta, 6.

13 Max Horkheimer, 'The Latest Attack on Metaphysics', in *Critical Theory: Selected Essays* (Seabury Press: New York), 132–87.

14 Ranajit Guha, 'On Some Aspects of the Historiography of Colonial India', *Subaltern Studies: Writings on South Asian History and Society* (New Delhi: Oxford University Press, 1982), 1–8.

15 Ashish Rajadhyaksha, 'Indian Cinema', in John Hill and Pamela Church Gibson (eds.), *The Oxford Guide to Film Studies* (Oxford: Oxford University Press, 1998), 535–40, 537.

16 M. Madhava Prasad, *Ideology of the Hindi Film: A Historical Construction* (New Delhi: Oxford University Press, 2001).

17 Datta, 32.

18 Datta, 60.

19 Van der Heide, 64.

20 Van der Heide, 3, quoting the former Indian prime minister Dr Manmohan Singh.

Chapter 1

1 Cross, 100.

2 Cross, 100, citing Sumita Chakravarty, *National Identity in Indian Popular Cinema 1947–1987* (Austin: University of Texas Press, 1993), 30.

3 Anuradha Dingwaney Needham, *New Indian Cinema in Post-Independence India: The Cultural Work of Shyam Benegal's Films* (New York: Routledge, 2013), 21.

4 Van der Heide, 57.

5 Datta, 64.

6 This passing reference does not do justice to the complex history of the nascent post-independence India, which, as Ramachandra Guha notes, remains largely unwritten. In *India after Gandhi: The History of the World's Largest Democracy* (New York: HarperCollins, 2007), Guha writes, 'The Republic of India is a union of twenty-eight states, some larger than France.

Yet not even the bigger or more important of these states have had their histories written.' Guha's own 'opus', cited above, runs to over 800 pages, and yet it is barely more than a sampler, an appetizer, a pointer to the many modern Indian histories that remain unwritten.

7 Dr Seuss, *Yertle the Turtle and Other Stories* (New York: Random House, 1958).

8 Datta, 70, citing M. Madhava Prasad, *The Ideology of the Hindi Film: A Historical Construction* (Oxford University Press, 2001).

9 Ashish Rajadhyaksha and Paul Willemen (eds.), *Encyclopaedia of Indian Cinema* (New Delhi: Oxford University Press, 2002), 416.

10 Cross, 90.

11 Needham, 60.

12 Screenplay and dialogue by Shyam Benegal and Satyadev Dubey.

13 Cross, 104.

14 Cross, 108.

15 Gayatri Spivak, 'Can the Subaltern Speak?' in Patrick Williams and Laura Chrisman (eds.), *Colonial Discourse and Post-Colonial Theory: A Reader* (New York: Harvester/Wheatsheaf, 1994), 66–111, emphasis in original.

16 Needham, 28.

17 Needham, 33.

18 Cross, 107.

19 Asha Kasbekar, 'Hidden Pleasures: Negotiating the Myth of the Female Ideal in Popular Hindi Cinema', in Rachel Dwyer and Christopher Pinney (eds.), *Pleasure and the Nation: The History, Politics and Consumption of Public Culture in India* (New Delhi and London: Oxford University Press, 2001), 286–308.

20 Catharine A. MacKinnon, 'Feminism, Marxism, Method, and the State: Toward Feminist Jurisprudence', *Signs*, 8, no. 4 (1983): 635–58.

21 Catherine Mackinnon, 'Reflections on Sex Equality under Law', *Yale Law Journal* 100, no. 5 (1991): 1212.

22 Cross, 108.

23 Needham, 29–30.

24 Needham, 30.

25 Needham, 30.

26 Needham, 31.

27 Needham, 32.

28 Needham, 37.

29 Sandra Lee Bartky, 'On Psychological Oppression', in Ann E. Cudd and Robin O. Andreasen (eds.), *Feminist Theory: A Philosophical Anthology* (Oxford: Blackwell Publishing, 2005), 105–14.

30 Needham, 42.

31 Needham, 42.

32 Friedrich Nietzsche, '"Guilt", "Bad Conscience" and the Like', *The Genealogy of Morals* (New York: Vintage, 1989).

33 Datta, 83.

34 Van der Heide, 71.

35 Needham, 41.

36 Needham, 39.

37 Needham, 44.

38 Elizabeth Frazer and Kimberly Hutchings, 'Argument and Rhetoric in the Justification of Political Violence', *European Journal of Political Theory* 6, no. 2 (2007): 180–99.

39 C. A. J. Coady, *Morality and Political Violence* (New York: Cambridge University Press, 2007), 22, citing Kenneth Grundy and Michael Weinstein, *The Ideologies of Violence* (Fulton, NY: Merrill, 1974), 8–13.

40 Ted Honderich, *Violence for Equality: Inquiries in Political Philosophy* (New York: Routledge, 1989).

41 Coady, 22.

42 Frantz Fanon, *The Wretched of the Earth* (Grove Press, 1963); see too Oladipo Fashina, 'Frantz Fanon and the Ethical Justification of Anti-Colonial Violence', *Social Theory and Practice* 15, no. 2 (1989): 179–212.

43 Fanon, 94.

44 Josh Pallas, Fanon on Violence and the Person, http://criticallegalthinking.com/2016/01/20/fanon-on-violence-and-the-person (accessed May 2019).

45 Fanon, 290.

46 Milkmen Turned Producers, https://www.thehindu.com/todays-paper/tp-features/tp-sundaymagazine/milkmen-turned-producers/article6181411.ece (accessed December 2019).

47 Screenplay and dialogue by Vijay Tendulkar and Kaifi Azmi.

48 Screenplay and dialogue by Vijay Tendulkar and Kaifi Azmi.

49 Here, Benegal offers homage to two Indian film classics that invoke the trope of the healing of a sick child by a supposed 'divine' as an act of building trust and establishing power: in Vijay Anand's 1965 *Guide*, Raju 'cures' a sick boy and is accepted as a saint by the village; in Satyajit Ray's 1960 *Devi*, the supposed 'goddess' cures a sick child, and becomes fatally convinced she is a 'goddess'. In both cases, 'promotion' to the divine is fatal as it is for the female protagonist in *Kondura*.

Chapter 2

1 Ann E. Cudd and Robin O. Andreasen, (eds.), *Feminist Theory: A Philosophical Anthology* (Oxford: Blackwell Publishing, 2005), 1–2.

2 Datta, 6.

3 Joan Wallach Scott, *Gender and the Politics of History* (New York: Columbia University Press, 1988), 17.

4 Datta, 198.

5 Cudd and Andreasen, 7.

6 Irene Gedalof, *Against Purity: Rethinking Identity with Indian and Western Feminisms* (New York: Routledge, 2005), 2, citing Teresa de Lauretis, 'Eccentric Subjects', *Feminist Studies* 16, no. 1 (1990): 115–50.

7 Gedalof, 30, citing Kumkum Sangari, 'Consent, Agency and Rhetorics of Incitement', *Economic and Political Weekly*, 1 May 1993, 867–82, 871.

8 Gedalof, 31, citing Gabriele Dietrich, 'Women and Religious Identities in India after Ayodhya', in K. Bhasin, R. Menon and N. Said Khan (eds.), *Against All Odds: Essays on Women, Religion and Development from India and Pakistan* (Delhi: Kali for Women, 1994), 35–49, 43–4.

9 Van der Heide, 63.

10 Uma Narayan, *Dislocating Cultures: Identities, Traditions, and Third World Feminism* (New York: Routledge, 1997), 9.

11 Narayan, 11–12.

12 Needham, 27.

13 Gedalof, 42, citing Uma Chakravarti, 'Whatever Happened to the Vedic Dasi?', in Kumkum Sangari and Sudesh Vaid (eds.), *Recasting Women: Essays in Indian Colonial History* (New Delhi: Kali for Women Press, 1989), 27–87.

14 In this tragic biographical detail, Wadkar is joined by Meena Kumari, a contemporaneous legendary actress of the Indian film industry, famous for her role in classic 'tragedies'. The contrast between Kumari's successful professional life and her failed personal one sparked popular speculation about the gap between the public and the private that resonates with the academic notes struck here. See, for instance, Baldev Chauhan, 'Meena Kumari the Melancholic Queen of Cinema!', at https://sunpost.in/meena-kumari-the-melancholic-queen-of-cinema/ (accessed May 2020).

15 Van der Heide, 87.

16 Susie Tharu and K. Lalita (eds.), *Women Writing in India Volume One, 600 BC to the Early Twentieth Century, Present* (New York: Feminist Press, 1991), 194.

17 Datta, 109.

18 Datta, 109.

19 Datta, 110–11.

20 Bartky, 'On Psychological Oppression', 105–14.

21 Van der Heide, 86; 'Interview with Shyam Benegal and Govind Nihalani', at https://www.youtube.com/watch?v=ylAVN17YUWQ; accessed December 2019.

22 Narayan, 53.

23 Van der Heide, 87–8.

24 Samir Chopra, *Bollywood Does Battle: The War Movie and the Indian Popular Imagination* (New Delhi: HarperCollins, forthcoming).

25 Martha Nussbaum, 'Women and Cultural Universals', in Maria Baghramian and Attracta Ingram (eds.), *Pluralism: The Philosophy and Politics of Diversity* (New York: Routledge, 2000).

26 Datta, 120–2.

27 Dungrus's anger at Rukmini could also be a function of his sexual denial and repression. The women of the brothel 'play' with Dungrus and treat him like a child, sometimes asking him to scrub their naked backs with soap but deny him indulgence in sexual favours. Dungrus is wholly desexualized in these encounters, and it is not entirely clear whether he is comfortable with this placement of his in the *mandi*; certainly, his mostly sullen expression indicates he is not.

28 Iris Marion Young, 'Five Faces of Oppression', from Lisa Heldke and Peg O'Connor (eds.), *Oppression, Privilege, and Resistance: Theoretical Perspectives on Racism, Sexism, and Heterosexism* (Boston: McGraw Hill, 2003), 37–63.

29 Van der Heide, 126.

30 Kate Millett, *Sexual Politics* (New York: Doubleday, 1970), 56.

31 Sylvia Vatuk, 'Islamic Feminism in India: Indian Muslim Women Activists and the Reform of Muslim Personal Law', *Modern Asian Studies* 42, nos. 2–3 (March 2008): 489–518.

32 Echoes of this debate occur in those between 'feminists of colour' and 'white liberal feminists': bell hooks, *Ain't I A Woman* (Boston: South End Press, 1981); *From Margin to Center* (Boston: South End Press, 1984); Cherrie Moraga and Gloria Anzaldua (eds.), *This Bridge Called My Back: Writings by Radical Women of Color* (New York: Kitchen Table/Women of Color Press, 1981); Valerie Amos and Pratibha Parmar, 'Challenging Imperial Feminism', in *Feminist Review* 17 (Autumn 1984): 3–19.

33 Gedalof, 9.

34 Urvashi Butalia, 'Community, State and Gender: On Women's Agency during Partition', *Economic and Political Weekly* 24 (April 1993): 12–24.

35 Narayan, 38.

36 Riyaz imagines his parents are both dead, but the truth about his father's behaviour is denied him by the protective Fayazi. When Riyaz does establish 'contact' with his father, he receives a cruel reply telling him not to write again, along with a check, because 'you must have written to ask for money'.

37 Annette C. Baier, 'The Need for More than Justice', *Canadian Journal of Philosophy* 17, no. 1 (1987): 41–56, quoting Carol Gilligan, *In a Different Voice* (Cambridge, MA: Harvard University Press, 1982).

38 Gilligan, 172.

39 Gilligan, 171.

40 Baier, 56.

Chapter 3

1 Datta, 130–1.

2 William Dalrymple, 'Believers and Infidels', in *The Last Mughal* (New York: Vintage, 2008).

3 Ruskin Bond, *Flight of Pigeons* (New Delhi: Penguin, 2007), 40.

4 Bond, 46.

5 Bond, 48.

6 Van der Heide, 150.

7 Screenplay and dialogues by Shyam Benegal, Satyadev Dubey and Ismat Chugtai.

8 Bond, 42.

9 Van der Heide, 99.

10 Datta, 212.

11 Van der Heide, 150.

12 This is another homage to Indian cinema: at last count, there were at least three separate versions of the Devdas legend that have found cinematic realization.

13 Narayan, 20.

14 William James, 'The Reality of the Unseen', from *The Varieties of Religious Experience: A Study in Human Nature* (New York: Penguin Classics, 1982).

15 Screenplay and dialogues by Aarudhra, Shyam Benegal and Girish Karnad.

16 Screenplay and dialogues by Aarudhra, Shyam Benegal and Girish Karnad.

17 Van der Heide, 113.

18 Van der Heide, 110.

19 Van der Heide, 109.

20 The story of Jamuna in *The Seventh Horse of the Sun* showed a similar reversal of the caste hierarchy by the love between Jamuna and the estate's caretaker. In both cases, it is sexual power that undermines the caste and class hierarchy.

21 Van der Heide, 105, citing Ashish Nandy, 'An Intelligent Critic's Guide to Indian Cinema', in *The Savage Freud and Other Essays on Possible and Retrievable Selves* (New Delhi: Oxford University Press), 196–236.

22 Herbert Marcuse, *One-Dimensional Man* (New York: Routledge Classics, 1964/2002).

23 The Indian invasion to 'liberate' Goa in December 1961 – after diplomatic negotiations to end Portuguese rule in Goa had failed – lasted a day. The tiny Portuguese garrison was overrun by Indian troops and surrendered quickly. India 'won' Goa but received considerable international criticism for its use of armed force, a tactic sharply contrasted with its public foreign policy stance of urging diplomacy on other nation states involved in similar imbroglios.

24 Screenplay and dialogues by Shyam Benegal and Shama Zaidi.

25 Datta, 143.

26 Gabriel Rockhill, 'Why We Never Die', at https://www.nytimes.com/2016/08/29/opinion/why-we-never-die.html (accessed December 2019).

27 Rockhill, 'Why We Never Die.'

28 Screenplay and dialogues by Shyam Benegal and Shama Zaidi.

29 Screenplay and dialogues by Shyam Benegal and Shama Zaidi.

30 In India, caste divisions are not exclusively a Hindu phenomenon and can be found in Sikhs, Muslims and Christians.

Conclusion

1 Datta, 235.

2 Van der Heide, 31.

3 Van der Heide, 31.

4 Van der Heide, 31.

5 Van der Heide, 33.

6 Ann E. Cudd and Leslie Jones, 'Sexism', in R. G. Frey and C. H. Wellman (eds.), *A Companion to Applied Ethics* (Oxford: Blackwell Publishers, 2003).

7 Young, 'Five Faces of Oppression', 37–63.

8 Marilyn Frye, 'Oppression', in *The Politics of Reality: Essays in Feminist Theory* (Trumansburg: Crossing Press, 1983).

9 Millett, 23.

10 Jean Grimshaw, 'Autonomy and Identity in Feminist Thinking', citing Mary Daly's 'Gyn/Ecology', in Morwenna Griffiths and Margaret Whitford (eds.), *Feminist Perspectives in Philosophy* (Indiana University Press, 1988), 90–108, 92.

11 Grimshaw, 92.

12 Catherine Mackinnon, 'Difference and Domination: On Sex Discrimination', in *Feminism Unmodified: Discourses on Life and Law* (Cambridge: Harvard University Press, 1987), 32–45, 45.

13 Sally Haslanger, 'Gender and Race: (What) Are They? (What) Do We Want Them To Be?' *Noûs* 34, no. 1 (2000): 31–55.

14 Gedalof, 11. Benegal thus engages with Luce Irigaray's claim that 'each woman's struggle will be different and will depend on which form of oppression is "for her most immediately unbearable"'. (c.f. Luce Irigaray, *This Sex Which Is Not One* (Ithaca: Cornell University Press, 1977), 166–7).

15 Marilyn Friedman, 'Autonomy, Social Disruption, and Women', from Catriona Mackenzie and Natalie Stoljar (eds.), *Relational Autonomy: Feminist Perspectives on Autonomy, Agency, and the Self* (New York City: Oxford University Press, 2000), 47.

16 Friedman, 49.

17 Friedman, 50.

18 Susan Okin, *Justice, Gender, and the Family* (New York: Basic Books, 1989).

19 Drucilla Cornell, 'Feminism, Utopianism, and the Role of the Ideal in Political Philosophy', in *At the Heart of Freedom: Feminism, Sex, and Equality* (Princeton, NJ: Princeton University Press, 1998), 174–86, 186.

20 Martha Minow, 'Words and the Door to the Land of Change: Law, Language, and Family Violence', 43 *Vanderbilt Law Review* 1665 (1990).

Bibliography

Amos, Valerie and Pratibha Parmar, 'Challenging Imperial Feminism', *Feminist Review* 17 (Autumn 1984): 3–19.

Arendt, Hannah, 'Thinking: Appearance and Semblance', in *The Life of the Mind*, vol. I, Harvest/HBJ, New York, 1981.

Bartky, Sandra Lee, 'On Psychological Oppression', in Ann E. Cudd and Robin Andreasen (eds.), *Feminist Theory: A Philosophical Anthology*, Blackwell Publishing, Oxford, 2005, pp. 105–14.

Bond, Ruskin, *Flight of Pigeons*, Penguin, New Delhi, 2007.

Bradatan, Costica, 'Philosophy Has a Lot to Learn from Film', https://aeon.co/ideas/philosophers-have-much-to-learn-from-the-great-filmmakers (accessed November 2019).

Butalia, Urvashi, 'Community, State and Gender: On Women's Agency during Partition', *Economic and Political Weekly*, 24 April 1993, pp. 12–24.

Chakravarti, Uma, 'Whatever Happened to the Vedic Dasi?', in Kumkum Sangari and Sudesh Vaid (eds.), *Recasting Women: Essays in Indian Cultural History*, Kali for Women, Delhi, 1989, pp. 27–87.

Chakravarty, Sumita, *National Identity in Indian Popular Cinema 1947–1987*, University of Texas Press, Austin, 1993.

Chopra, Samir, *Bollywood Goes to War: The Indian War Movie*, HarperCollins, forthcoming.

Coady, C. A. J., *Morality and Political Violence*, Cambridge University Press, New York, 2007.

Cornell, Drucilla, 'Feminism, Utopianism, and the Role of the Ideal in Political Philosophy', in *At the Heart of Freedom: Feminism, Sex, and Equality*, Princeton University Press, 1998, pp. 174–86.

Cross, Robert, 'Shyam Benegal's Ankur and the Nehruvian Woman', *Doshisha Studies in Language and Culture*, 13, no. 2 (2010): 89–115.

Cudd, Ann E. and Robin O. Andreasen, (eds.), *Feminist Theory: A Philosophical Anthology*, Blackwell Publishing, Oxford, 2005.

Dalrymple, William, 'Believers and Infidels', in *The Last Mughal*, Vintage, New York, 2008.

Datta, Sangeeta, *Shyam Benegal*, Rolli Books, New Delhi, 2005.

Dietrich, Gabriele, 'Women and Religious Identities in India after Ayodhya', in K. Bhasin, R. Menon and N. Said Khan (eds.), *Against All Odds: Essays on Women, Religion and Development from India and Pakistan*, Kali for Women, Delhi, 1994, pp. 35–49.

Fanon, Frantz, *The Wretched of the Earth*, Grove Press, New York, 1963.

Fashina, Oladipo, 'Fanon, Frantz and the Ethical Justification of Anti-Colonial Violence', *Social Theory and Practice*, 15, no. 2 (1989): 179–212.

Frazer, Elizabeth and Kimberly Hutchings, 'Argument and Rhetoric in the Justification of Political Violence', *European Journal of Political Theory*, 6, no. 2 (2007): 180–99.

Friedman, Marilyn, 'Autonomy, Social Disruption, and Women', from Catriona Mackenzie and Natalie Stoljar (eds.), *Relational Autonomy: Feminist Perspectives on Autonomy, Agency, and the Self*, Oxford University Press, New York City, 2000.

Gedalof, Irene, *Against Purity: Rethinking Identity with Indian and Western Feminisms*, Routledge, New York, 2005.

Geuss, Raymond, *Philosophy and Real Politics*, Princeton University Press, Princeton, 2008.

Gilligan, Carol, *In a Different Voice*, Harvard University Press, Cambridge, MA, 1982.

Grimshaw, Jean, 'Autonomy and Identity in Feminist Thinking', citing Mary Daly's 'Gyn/Ecology', in Morwenna Griffiths and Margaret Whitford (eds.), *Feminist Perspectives in Philosophy*, Indiana University Press, Bloomington, 1988, pp. 90–108.

Grundy, Kenneth and Michael Weinstein, *The Ideologies of Violence*, Merrill, New York City, 1974, pp. 8–13.

Guha, Ramachandra, *India after Gandhi: The History of the World's Largest Democracy*, HarperCollins, New York City, 2007.

Guha, Ranajit, 'On Some Aspects of the Historiography of Colonial India', In *Subaltern Studies: Writings on South Asian History and Society*, Oxford University Press, New Delhi, 1982, pp. 1–8.

Haslanger, Sally, 'Gender and Race: (What) Are They? (What) Do We Want Them to Be?' *Noûs*, 34, no. 1 (2000): 31–55.

Heide, William van der, *Bollywood Babylon: Interviews with Shyam Benegal*, Bloomsbury, New York, 2006, pp. 24–7.

Honderich, Ted, *Violence for Equality: Inquiries in Political Philosophy*, Routledge, New York, 1989.

hooks, bell, *Ain't I A Woman*, South End Press, Boston, 1981; *From Margin to Center*, South End Press, Boston, 1984.

Horkheimer, Max, 'The Latest Attack on Metaphysics', *Critical Theory: Selected Essays*, Seabury Press, pp. 132–87.

'Interview with Shyam Benegal and Govind Nihalani', at https://www.youtube.com/watch?v=ylAVN17YUWQ (accessed December 2019).

Irigaray, Luce, *This Sex Which Is Not One*, Cornell University Press, Ithaca, 1977, pp. 166–7.

James, William, 'The Reality of the Unseen', from *The Varieties of Religious Experience: A Study in Human Nature*, Penguin Classics, New York, 1982.

Kasbekar, Asha, 'Hidden Pleasures: Negotiating the Myth of the Female Ideal in Popular Hindi Cinema', in Rachel Dwyer and Christopher Pinney (eds.), *Pleasure and the Nation: The History, Politics and Consumption of Public Culture in India*, Oxford University Press, New Delhi and London, 2001, pp. 286–308.

Krishen, Pradip, 'Knocking at the Doors of Public Culture: India's Parallel Cinema', *Public Culture*, 4, no. 1 (1991): 24–41.

Lauretis, Teresa de, 'Eccentric Subjects', *Feminist Studies*, 16, no. 1 (1990): 115–50.

Mackinnon, Catherine, 'Difference and Domination: On Sex Discrimination', in *Feminism Unmodified: Discourses on Life and Law*, Harvard University Press, Cambridge, 1987, pp. 32–45.

MacKinnon, Catharine A., 'Feminism, Marxism, Method, and the State: Toward Feminist Jurisprudence', *Signs*, 8, no. 4 (1983): 635–58.

Mackinnon, Catherine, 'Reflections on Sex Equality under Law', *Yale Law Journal*, 100, no. 5 (1991): 1212.

Magee, Bryan, *Confessions of a Philosopher*, Random House, New York, 1997.

Marcuse, Herbert, *One-Dimensional Man*, Routledge Classics, New York, 1964/2002.

Milkmen Turned Producers, https://www.thehindu.com/todays-paper/tp-features/tp-sundaymagazine/milkmen-turned-producers/article6181411.ece (accessed December 2019).

Millett, Kate, *Sexual Politics*, Doubleday, New York, 1970.

Minow, Martha, 'Words and the Door to the Land of Change: Law, Language, and Family Violence', 43 *Vanderbilt Law Review* (1990): 1665.

Moraga, Cherrie and Gloria Anzaldua, (eds.), *This Bridge Called My Back: Writings by Radical Women of Color*, Kitchen Table/Women of Color Press, New York, 1981.

Mulhall, Stephen, *On Film*, Routledge, New York, 2001.

Nandy, Ashish, 'An Intelligent Critic's Guide to Indian Cinema', in *The Savage Freud and Other Essays on Possible and Retrievable Selves*, Oxford University Press, New Delhi, pp. 196–236.

Narayan, Uma, *Dislocating Cultures: Identities, Traditions, and Third World Feminism*, Routledge, New York, 1997.

Needham, Anuradha Dingwaney, *New Indian cinema in Post-Independence India: The Cultural Work of Shyam Benegal's Films*, Routledge, New York, 2013.

Nietzsche, Friedrich, '"Guilt", "Bad Conscience" and The Like', *The Genealogy of Morals*, Vintage, New York, 1989.

Nussbaum, Martha, 'Women and Cultural Universals', in Maria Baghramian and Attracta Ingram, (eds.), *Pluralism: The Philosophy and Politics of Diversity*, Routledge, New York, 2000.

Okin, Susan, *Justice, Gender, and the Family*, Basic Books, New York, 1989.

Pallas, Josh, 'Fanon on Violence and the Person', http://criticallegalthinking.com/2016/01/20/fanon-on-violence-and-the-person (accessed May 2019).

Prasad, M. Madhava, *Ideology of the Hindi Film: A Historical Construction*, Oxford University Press, 2001.

Rajadhyaksha, Ashish, 'Indian Cinema', in John Hill and Pamela Church Gibson (eds.), *The Oxford Guide to Film Studies*, Oxford University Press, Oxford, 1998, pp. 535–40.

Rajadhyaksha, Ashish and Paul Willemen (eds.), *Encyclopaedia of Indian Cinema*, Oxford University Press, New Delhi, 2002.

Rockhill, Gabriel, 'Why We Never Die', at https://www.nytimes.com/2016/08/29/opinion/why-we-never-die.html (accessed December 2019).

Sangari, Kumkum, 'Consent, Agency and Rhetorics of Incitement', *Economic and Political Weekly*, 1 May 1993, pp. 867–82.

Scott, Joan Wallach, *Gender and the Politics of History*, Columbia University Press, New York, 1988.

Spivak, Gayatri, "Can the Subaltern Speak?" in Patrick Williams and Laura Chrisman (eds.), *Colonial Discourse and Post-Colonial Theory: A Reader*, Harvester/Wheatsheaf, New York, 1994, pp. 66–111.

Tharu, Susie and K. Lalita (eds.), *Women Writing in India Volume One, 600 BC to the Early Twentieth Century*, Present, Feminist Press, New York, 1991.

Vatuk, Sylvia, 'Islamic Feminism in India: Indian Muslim Women Activists and the Reform of Muslim Personal Law', *Modern Asian Studies*, 42, 2–3 (March 2008) :489–518.

Young, Iris Marion, "Five Faces of Oppression," in Lisa Heldke and Peg O'Connor (eds.), *Oppression, Privilege, & Resistance: Theoretical Perspectives on Racism, Sexism, and Heterosexism*, McGraw Hill, Boston, 2003, pp. 37–63.

Index

Note: Page numbers followed by "n" refer to notes.